# Read Greek by Friday

## Creative Tools for Learning

En arch
hn
o logo~

*including Crossword Puzzles, Songs, Games, & More*

**Paul Fullmer**

WIPF & STOCK PUBLISHERS
EUGENE OREGON

**Wipf and Stock Publishers**
**199 West 8th Avenue**
**Eugene, Oregon 97401**
**Www.wipfandstock.com**

Read Greek by Friday: Creative Tools for Learning
By Paul Fullmer

ISBN: 1-59244-773-2



The author gratefully acknowledges express permission to reproduce the following images and texts:
Information for "Correlative Bingo" (page 23) courtesy of the University of California Press;
Header art (pages 50, 53, 54) courtesy of A.G. Green, holy_orthodox.tripod.com;
Header art (pages 51, 52) courtesy of "Clipart.com."

# Table of Contents

# Table of Contents (2)

# Introduction

At the annual meeting of the Biblical Greek Language Section of the Society of Biblical Literature, the question seems to arise anew each year: "I'm looking for a book of creative resources for teaching Greek. Does anyone know of one?" Another instructor with a new appointment to teach New Testament Greek seeks to liven up a course often stigmatized as extremely difficult and frustrating for students.

This book, a companion volume to *Read Greek by Friday: A Beginning Grammar and Exercises*, provides such resources. Memory devices, creative learning experiences (songs, crossword puzzles, and flowcharts), and additional exercises enhance initial encounters with Greek grammar and vocabulary, easing the transition to the reading of Greek texts.

The vocabulary crossword puzzles, for example, provide a creative means of reviewing the vocabulary lists in the *Beginning Grammar and Exercises* as well as the additional vocabulary lists in this volume. The puzzles are not only entertaining in and of themselves, but – more importantly – they reinforce vocabulary for an even more exciting process: the reading of the Greek texts.

The initial inspiration for this volume derives from the enthusiastic and animated instruction of Sam Gantt at Fuller Theological Seminary. Sam's vibrant teaching was full of creativity, song, and spirituality. I am particularly indebted to Sam for concepts behind the development of the "Parsing Flow Chart" on page 37.

Robert Smith evoked my own initial attempts at creativity when I served as Teaching Assistant for the Summer Biblical Greek Program at the Pacific Lutheran Theological Seminary (PLTS). He asked me to develop an engaging way for students to learn vocabulary. The result was not only the development of a set of crossword puzzles, but several years of creative thinking about how to engage students with the Greek language. Both he and Everett Kalin, also at PLTS, were a kind audience as I tried out my own songs, crosswords, and group games. Thank you!

Several professors at the University of California at Berkeley have been instrumental in developing my love for Greek. Leslie Threatte has been both a constant resource and a friend throughout my doctoral studies. Greek gaming is the brainchild of G.R.F. Ferrari, also at UC Berkeley. (See pages 55-59.)

In short, this handbook seeks to make learning Greek a positive experience. I believe that if students have an agreeable – even fun! – experience in an elementary Greek course, they will be all the more likely to continue work with the language beyond the initial encounter.

Paul Fullmer
Ph. D. Candidate at
The Graduate Theological Union
Berkeley, California

# HELP WITH THE ALPHABET
## AND THE DEFINITE ARTICLE

*Writing the Alphabet: A Reproducible Sheet*
*Crossword: People and Places*
*The Alphabet Song*
*Twinkle, Twinkle Little Definite Article*

## Writing The Alphabet: A Reproducible Sheet

Practice writing out the letters of the Greek alphabet. Make additional copies of this page before you do if you think you might benefit from more than one review.

## Crossword: People & Places

Because the Greek words below consist entirely of proper names, they can be "translated" into English without the help of a dictionary.

Practice your knowledge of the Greek alphabet by reading these words aloud, determining the English equivalent, and writing that English equivalent in the crossword puzzle.

**Across**

4. Libuh
6. Aqhnai
7. Iskariwq
8. Artemi~
11. Agar
14. Galilaia
18. Ioudaia
19. Naqanahl
21. Wshe
23. Sousanna
24. Samareia
26. Barqolomaio~
29. Fhlix
32. Aristarco~
34. Stefano~
35. Agrippa~
37. Aigupto~
39. Rouq
41. Ierosoluma
42. Korinqo~

**Down**

1. Suntuch
2. Rodh
3. Mwush~
5. Marqa
9. Xloh
10. Iwshf
12. Geqshmani
13. Faraw
15. Alexandro~
16. Cristo~
17. Gabrihl
20. Nikodhmo~
22. Zakcaio~
25. Ihsou~
26. Bhqleem
27. Louka~
28. Micahl
30. Hsaia~
31. Barnaba~
33. Israhl
36. Paulo~
38. Petro~
39. Rwmh
40. Siwn

# The Alphabet Song

Here's a song to help you memorize the alphabet. The tune is from the traditional favorite "Mary Had a Little Lamb."

Having a strong grasp of the alphabet and its order will be particularly helpful for referencing a Greek dictionary. Time invested in learning the alphabet now will certainly reap a generous return!

## Twinkle, Twinkle, Little Definite Article

People learn in lots of different ways.

If you like music, learn by association, or frequently travel a long commute, you might enjoy learning the definite article to the tune of “Twinkle, Twinkle, Little Star.”

Whether this is helpful for you or not, learning the forms of the definite article will greatly enhance your enjoyment of Greek. Work to learn these forms now and you’ll be repaid generously with much greater ease in reading!

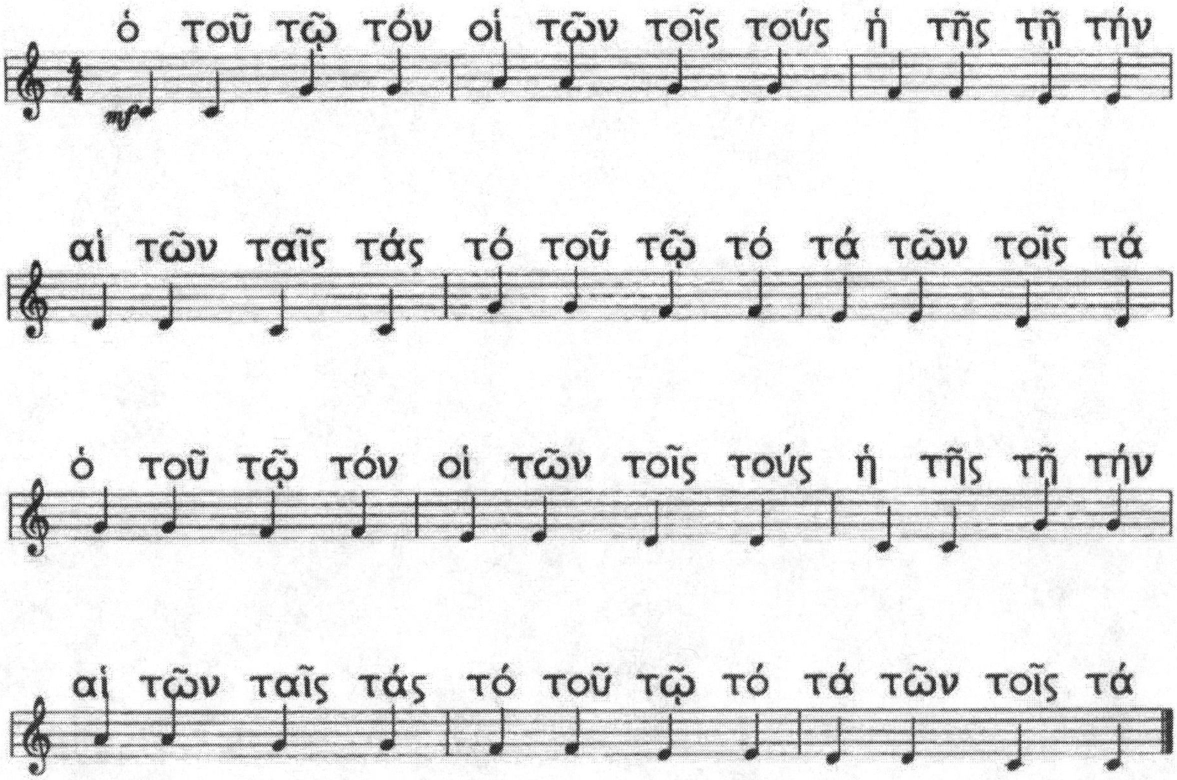


PARADIGM: THE DEFINITE ARTICLE

| | Masculine | Feminine | Neuter |
|---|---|---|---|
| **N**omitive | ὁ | ἡ | τό |
| **G**enitive | τοῦ | τῆς | τοῦ |
| **D**ative | τῷ | τῇ | τῷ |
| **A**ccusative | τόν | τήν | τό |
| **N**ominative | οἱ | αἱ | τά |
| **G**enitive | τῶν | τῶν | τῶν |
| **D**ative | τοῖς | ταῖς | τοῖς |
| **A**ccusative | τούς | τάς | τά |

# HELP WITH VOCABULARY

*Making Vocabulary Cards: 7 Easy Steps*
*Additional Vocabulary Lists*
*Vocabulary Crossword Puzzles*
*Some Big Little "o" Words:* οὐ *&* ὅτι
*Correlatives ("Correlative Bingo")*

## Making Vocabulary Cards: 7 Easy Steps

Getting an early start on flashcards will greatly facilitate vocabulary learning. The system described here is flexible, portable, and affordable!

1. Cut several lined 3" x 5" index cards in half.
2. On the blank ("front") side write the dictionary form of the word you will memorize.
3. Is the word you are learning a noun or adverb? If so, write the genitive ending and the corresponding article on the top line of the opposite ("back") side of the card. On the second line, write the most basic meaning of the word. (See example below.)
4. If the word is a verb, number the bottom lines of the back side of the card from 2 – 6, as illustrated below. Write out the corresponding "principal parts" for the verb on these lines. You'll find all the "Principal Parts" you will need for this course included in the section of "Vocabulary" near the end of the book. Don't worry about learning all of these parts just yet. For now, focus on learning the basic meaning of the verb. As you continue to learn Greek, you'll come to appreciate this aspect of your vocabulary cards more and more.
5. Use the lines between the basic meaning and any principal parts to list any verbs or nouns related to the word on the front side of the card.
6. If you find more cognates, write them on another half-card and staple it to the front of the card you have, keeping the principal parts on the last card.
7. Stash your cards in a purse or pocket for the next time you must wait patiently in line. You'll be glad you did!

***Sample Noun/Adverb Card***

Front:

adelfo~

Back:

-ou o
brother

***Sample Verb Card***

Front:

ballw

Back:

throw
diaballw slander
diabolh, h slander
ekballw drive out
periballw clothe
2) balew
3) ebalon
4) beblhka
5) beblhmai
6) eblhqhn

# Additional Vocabulary Lists 16-21

**List #16**
allhlwn one another
apodidwmi I give back; middle: I sell
glwssa tongue, language
dexio~, -a, -on right
dwdeka twelve
eite... eite either... or
erw future of legw (speak, say)
liqo~, -ou o stone
mero~, merou~ to part
peirazw I try, tempt
presbutero~, -h, -on older
oligo~, -h, -on few, little
ouketi no longer
swthria, -a~ h salvation
trito~, -h, -on third

**List #17**
aspazomai I greet
dikaiosunh, -h~ h righteousness, justice
dio therefore
emo~, -h, -on my
eti still, yet
euaggelizw I preach, proclaim good news
hdh already
qerapeuw I heal
lao~, -ou o people
loipo~, -h, -on remaining
ote when
prosferw I bring to, offer
upostrefw I return
fanerow I reveal
fobo~, -ou o fear

**List #18**
agro~, -ou o field
amartanw I sin
erhmo~, -on deserted
h or, than
qalassa, -h~ h sea
imation, -ou to outer garment
marturia testimony, witness
martu~, marturo~ o witness
otan whenever
planaw I lead astray
probaton, -ou to sheep
proswpon, -ou to face
pur, puro~ to fire
telo~, telou~ to end
cwri~ G: without, apart from

**List #19**
arti now
blasfhmew I blaspheme, revile
deutero~, -a, -on second
eto~, etou~ to year
kaqizw I sit
kako~, -h, -on bad, evil
lalew I speak
ou~, wto~ to ear
oute... oute neither... nor
ofeilw I owe, ought
parabolh, -h~ h parable
shmeron today
toiouto~, -h, -on such a one
tote then
trei~, tria three

**List #20**
amartwlo~, -h, -on sinful
acri (acri~) until G: as far as;
didaskalo~, -ou o teacher
ekasto~, -h, -on each
emprosqen G: in front of, before
etero~, -h, -on other
klaiw I weep
kratew I seize, grasp
luw I loose, release, destroy
mikro~, -a, -on small, little
oikodomew I build
paralambanw I receive
ptwco~, -h, -on poor
timh, -h~ h honor, price
wsper just as

**List #21**
arcwn, arconto~ o ruler
asqenew I am weak
boulomai I wish, want
eggizw I come near, approach
elpi~, elpido~ h hope
enwpion in the presence of
exw outside, outer nao~, -ou o temple
kaino~, -h, -on new
orgh, -h~ h anger
ouai woe!
paraginomai I arrive, come
pascw I suffer
sofia, sofia~ h wisdom
staurow I crucify
creia, -a~ h a need

# Additional Vocabulary Lists 22-25

**List #22**

apa~, apasa, apan all
genea, -a~ h generation
dew I bind
epaggelia, -a~ h promise
epiginwskw I recognize
epta seven
qaumazw I marvel, wonder at
mallon more, rather
men on the one hand, but
mhthr, mhtro~ h mother
opw~ so that; adv: how
oro~, orou~ to mountain
osti~, hti~, oti whoever, whatever
perisseuw I abound, am rich
sperma, spermato~ to seed

**List #23**

ara then, therefore
dunami~, -ew~ h power, ability
euqu~ immediately
ew~ till, until
qhrion, -ou to wild beast
qliyi~, -ew~ h tribulation
krisi~, krisew~ h judgment
pleiwn, pleiono~ more
pou where?
pro G: before
rhma, rhmato~ to word
stoma, stomato~ to mouth
te and
fulakh, -h~ h guard, prison, watch (of time)
w~ as, when, about
wde here

**List #24**

axio~, -a, -on worthy
aptw burn, kindle; middle: touch
diwkw I pursue, persecute
epiqumia, -a~ h passion, desire
ergazomai I work
etoimazw I prepare
eucaristew I give thanks
qura, -a~ h door
ikano~, -h, on enough, sufficient
katoikew I inhabit, dwell
omoio~, -a, -on like
prassw I do, perform
pantote always
fwnew I call

**List #25**

anastasi~, -ew~ h resurrection
dikaiow I justify, pronounce righteous
logizomai I narrate, account
misew I hate
doulo~, -ou o slave
mnhmeion, -ou to tomb, monument
paristhmi I am present
diabolo~, -on slandering
diakonew I serve, minister to
eulogew I bless
epistrefw I return, I turn to
kalw~ well
metanoew I repent
opisw G: behind, after
upotassw I subject, put into subjection

# Crossword Puzzle: Vocabulary Lists 1-3

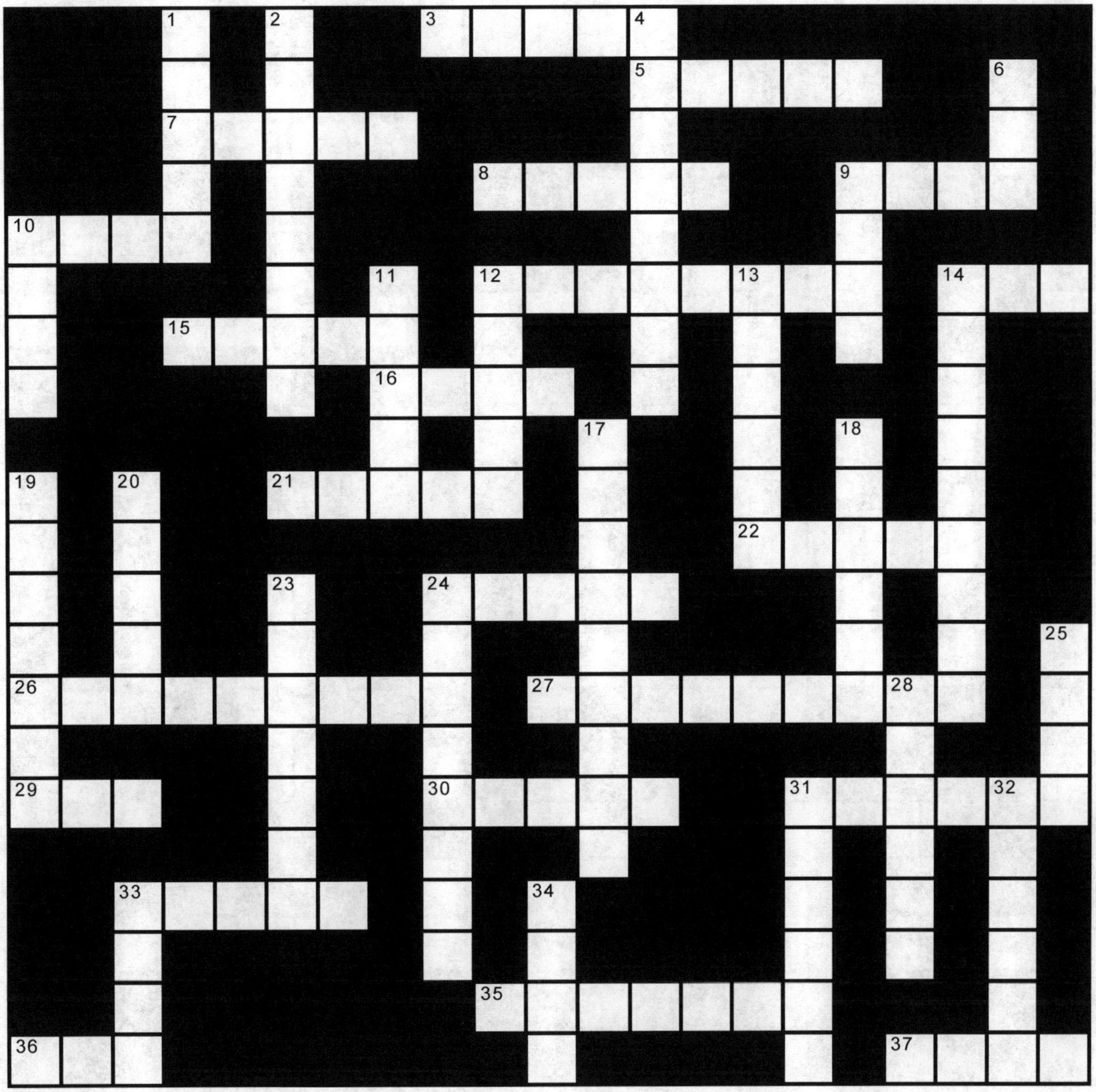

**Across**

**3.** oclo~
**5.** swzw
**7.** ecw
**8.** topo~
**9.** legw
**10.** logo~
**12.** baptizw
**14.** uio~
**15.** alhqeia
**16.** ponhro~
**21.** kosmo~
**22.** kardia
**24.** pempw
**26.** sunagwgh
**27.** khrussw
**29.** hmera
**30.** agw
**31.** krinw
**33.** doxa
**35.** profhth~
**36.** qeo~
**37.** agio~

**Down**

**1.** teknon
**2.** ekballw
**4.** maqhth~
**6.** odo~
**9.** blepw
**10.** ergon
**11.** akouw
**12.** euriskw
**13.** didaskw
**14.** grafh
**17.** apostellw
**18.** ourano~
**19.** makario~
**20.** anqrwpo~
**23.** adelfo~
**24.** pisteuw
**25.** zwh
**28.** ekklhsia
**31.** grafw
**32.** euaggelion
**33.** agaqo~
**34.** kurio~

# Crossword Puzzle: Vocabulary Lists 4-6

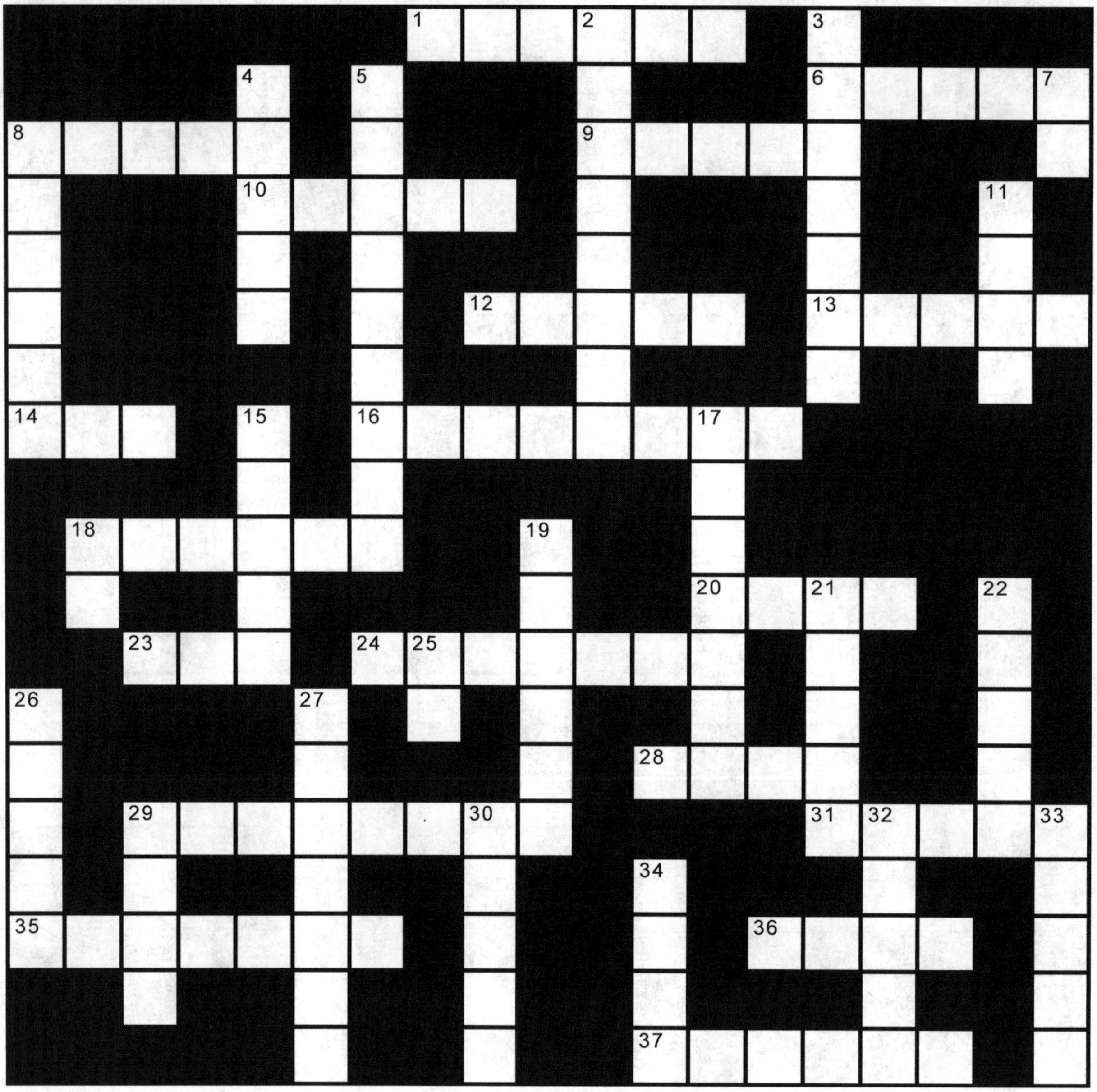

**Across**

1. egeirw
6. ginwskw
8. qelw
9. anoigw
10. aggelo~
12. paidion
13. ek
14. o~
16. peiqw
18. ferw
20. outo~
23. ei~
24. dia
28. apo
29. katabainw
31. gh
35. oude
36. sun
37. pro~

**Down**

2. apoluw
3. basileia
4. lambanw
5. arch
7. hmei~
8. ballw
11. epi
15. fwnh
17. sunagw
18. en
19. peri
21. ercomai
22. karpo~
25. auto~
26. daimonion
27. anabainw
29. ei~
30. oudei~
32. meta
33. oikia
34. ekeino~

# Crossword Puzzle: Vocabulary Lists 7-9

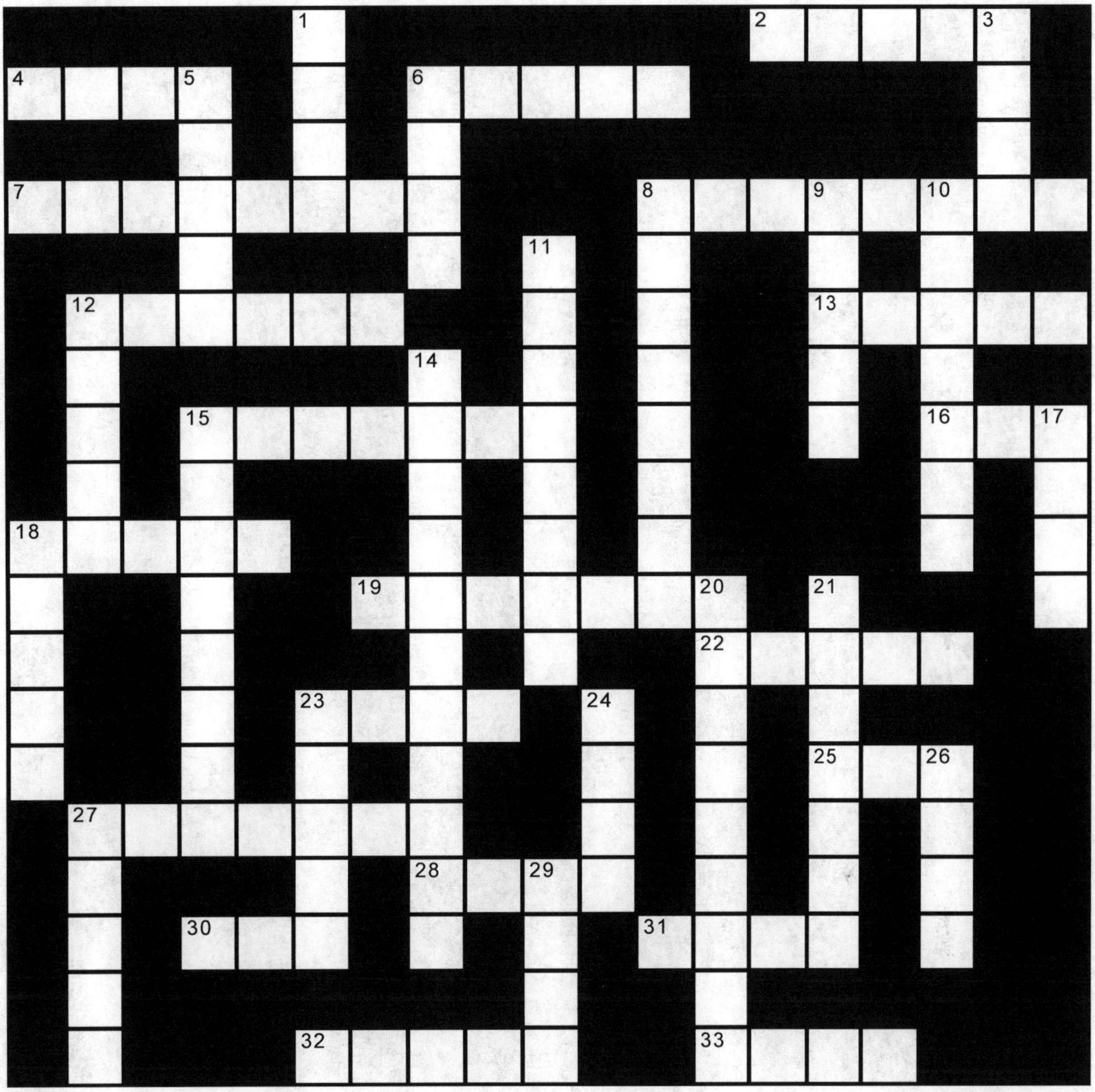

**Across**
**2.** oida
**4.** basileu~
**6.** agapaw
**7.** oso~
**8.** plhrow
**12.** gennaw
**13.** mega~
**15.** krazw
**16.** pa~
**18.** threw
**19.** apokrinomai
**22.** arcw
**23.** swma
**25.** kako~
**27.** ginomai
**28.** onoma
**30.** de
**31.** kalo~
**32.** sarx
**33.** shmeion

**Down**
**1.** poli~
**3.** qelhma
**5.** cari~
**6.** erwtaw
**8.** cairw
**9.** fw~
**10.** menw
**11.** marturew
**12.** peripatew
**14.** entolh
**15.** decomai
**17.** agaph
**18.** zhtew
**20.** dikaio~
**21.** anhr
**23.** aima
**24.** oraw
**26.** kata
**27.** kalew
**29.** polu~

# Crossword Puzzle: Vocabulary Lists 10-12

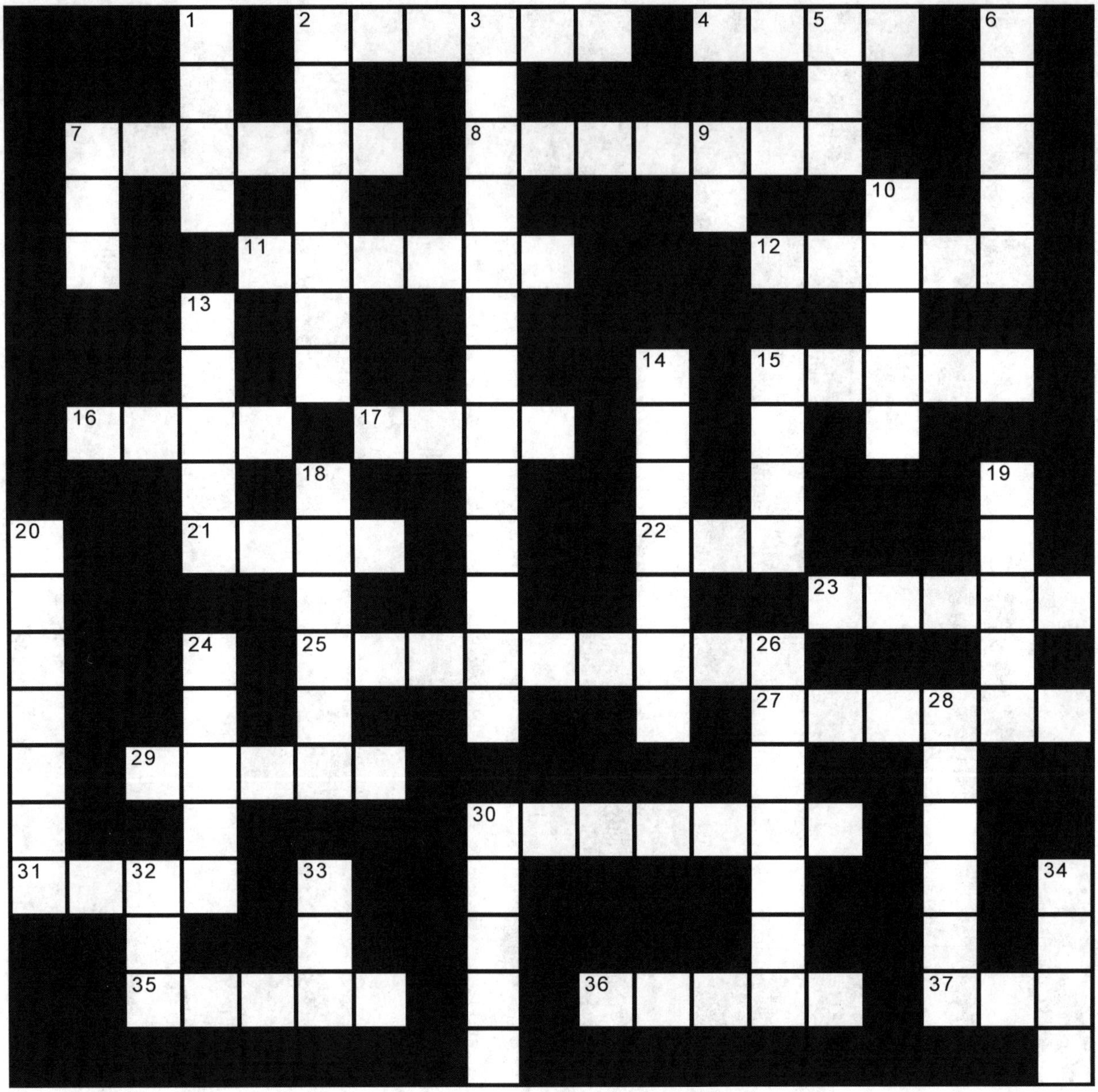

**Across**

**2.** pinw
**4.** nekro~
**7.** pneuma
**8.** dunamai
**11.** dokew
**12.** qelw
**15.** fobeomai
**16.** esqiw
**17.** qewrew
**21.** wra
**22.** nomo~
**23.** arto~
**25.** wste
**27.** ieron
**29.** prwto~
**30.** apercomai
**31.** ceir
**35.** opou
**36.** apokteinw
**37.** duo

**Down**

**1.** apoqnhskw
**2.** airw
**3.** dei
**5.** aiwn
**6.** nux
**7.** amartia
**9.** upo
**10.** udwr
**13.** qanato~
**14.** akolouqew
**15.** speirw
**18.** kaqw~
**19.** kalew
**20.** sabbaton
**24.** tuflo~
**26.** aiwnio~
**28.** iereu~
**30.** zaw
**32.** nun
**33.** gar
**34.** pou~

# Crossword Puzzle: Vocabulary Lists 13-15

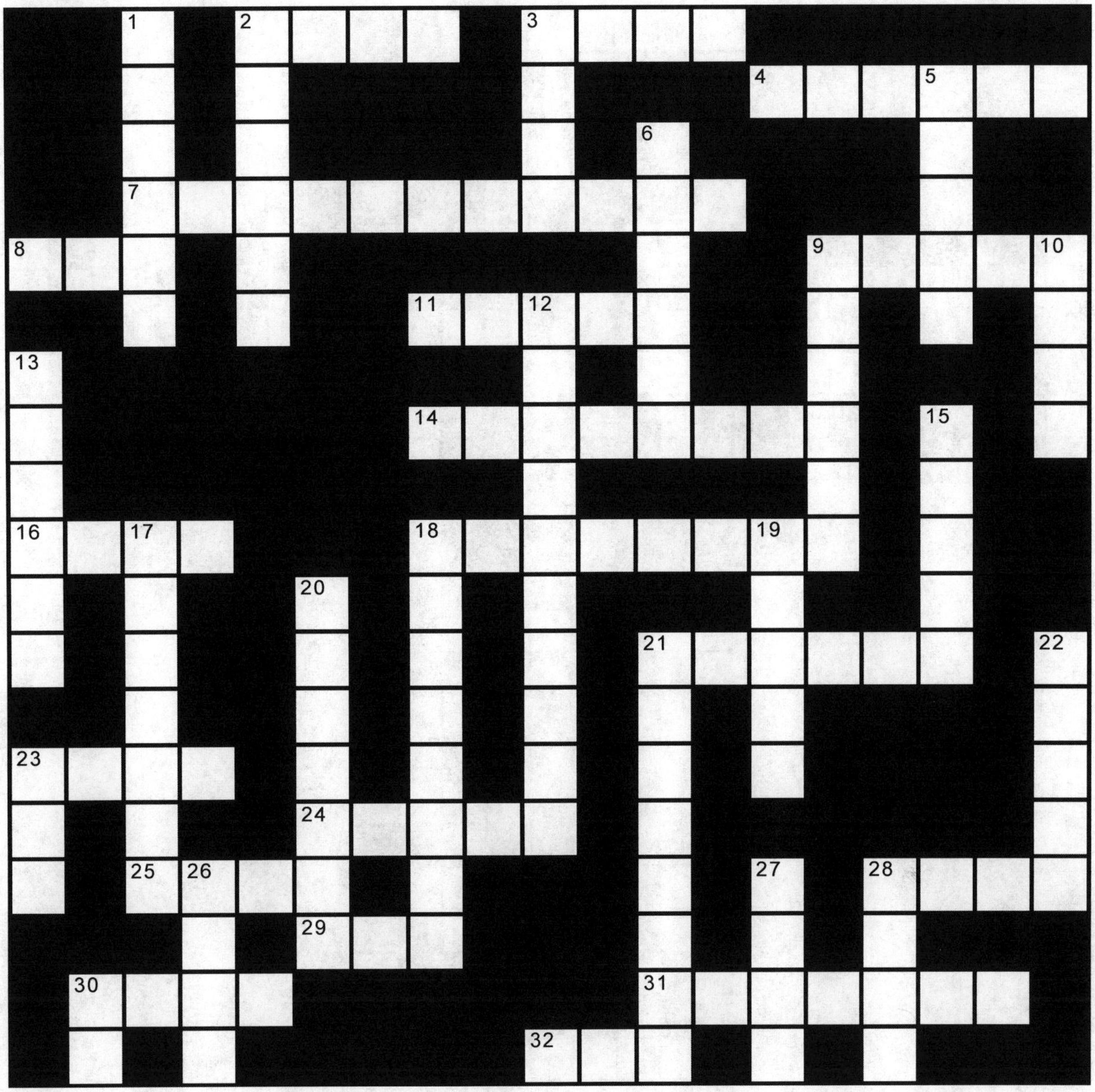

**Across**

**2.** crono~
**3.** aitew
**4.** uparcw
**7.** ina
**8.** poreuomai
**9.** piptw
**11.** pisti~
**14.** paradidwmi
**16.** kaqhmai
**18.** proskunew
**21.** anisthmi
**23.** ploion
**24.** didwmi
**25.** outw~
**28.** yuch
**29.** ofqalmo~
**30.** fhmi
**31.** idio~
**32.** cara

**Down**

**1.** eqno~
**2.** qrono~
**3.** tiqhmi
**5.** proseucomai
**6.** pathr
**9.** isthmi
**10.** escato~
**12.** parakalew
**13.** grammateu~
**15.** eirhnh
**17.** upagw
**18.** afihmi
**19.** peripatew
**20.** doxazw
**21.** apollumi
**22.** olo~
**23.** alla
**26.** kefalh
**27.** oun
**28.** idou
**30.** ei

# Jumbo Crossword for Review: Vocabulary Lists 1-15

**Across**

**1.** doxazw
**4.** pneuma
**6.** sunagwgh
**8.** poreuomai
**11.** pa~
**12.** eqno~
**13.** gar
**14.** su
**15.** dikaio~
**19.** parakalew
**22.** aiwn
**23.** cairw
**25.** logo~
**26.** apokrinomai
**29.** dunamai
**31.** ofqalmo~
**33.** agaqo~
**35.** crono~
**37.** de
**38.** duo
**40.** o~
**43.** auto~
**44.** onoma
**45.** pro~

**Down**

**1.** ecw
**2.** apostolo~
**3.** grafh
**5.** alhqeia
**6.** amartia
**7.** oude
**8.** apoqnhskw
**9.** cara
**10.** krinw
**11.** peri
**16.** euaggelion
**17.** outo~
**18.** ei~
**19.** ei
**20.** nun
**21.** oso~
**24.** en
**27.** fwnh
**28.** meso~
**30.** fw~
**32.** umei~
**34.** swma
**36.** ei~
**39.** allo~
**41.** ceir
**42.** alla
**43.** pw~

# Crossword Puzzle: Vocabulary Lists 16-18

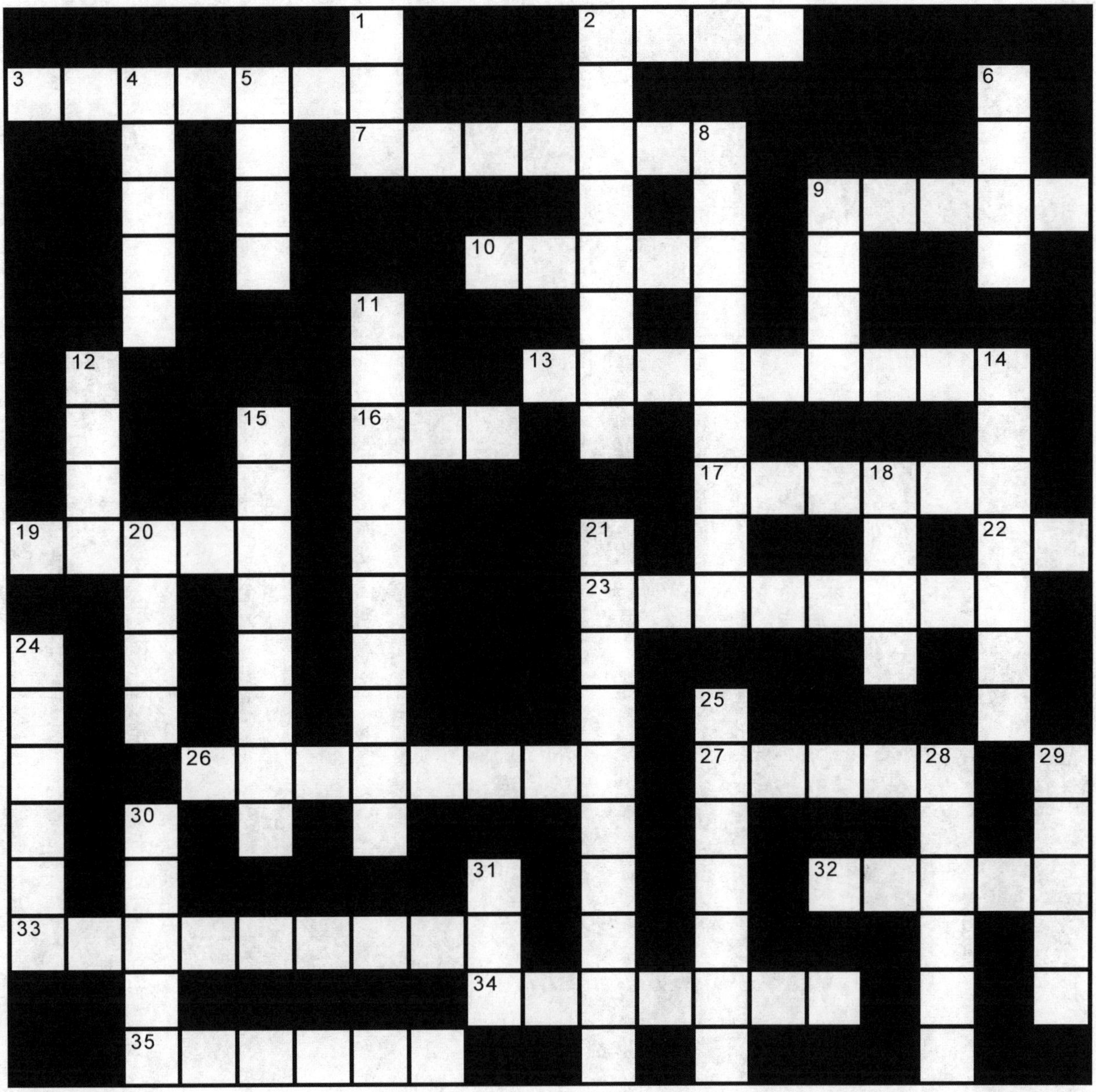

**Across**

**2.** ote
**3.** dikaiosunh
**7.** martu~
**9.** trito~
**10.** qerapeuw
**13.** loipo~
**16.** telo~
**17.** prosferw
**19.** eti
**22.** emo~
**23.** glwssa
**26.** erhmo~
**27.** dexio~
**32.** agro~
**33.** dio
**34.** hdh
**35.** lao~

**Down**

**1.** oligo~
**2.** otan
**4.** liqo~
**5.** amartanw
**6.** pur
**8.** swthria
**9.** h
**11.** allhlwn
**12.** mero~
**14.** imation
**15.** ouketi
**18.** fobo~
**20.** peirazw
**21.** planaw
**24.** aspazomai
**25.** fanerow
**28.** dwdeka
**29.** presbutero~
**30.** probaton
**31.** qalassa

# Crossword Puzzle: Vocabulary Lists 19-21

**Across**

**1.** deutero~
**2.** kaqizw
**4.** wsper
**6.** timh
**7.** arti
**8.** eto~
**9.** kaino~
**11.** acri
**13.** creia
**14.** orgh
**15.** parabolh
**16.** ofeilw
**17.** luw
**19.** etero~
**20.** paraginomai
**22.** boulomai
**24.** trei~
**25.** ou~
**26.** kratew
**29.** blasfhmew
**31.** shmeron
**32.** arcwn
**33.** ekasto~

**Down**

**1.** amartwlo~
**2.** pascw
**3.** tote
**5.** mikro~
**10.** ouai
**12.** didaskalo~
**13.** oute
**15.** ptwco~
**18.** toiouto~
**19.** exw
**21.** staurow
**22.** lalew
**23.** klaiw
**27.** oikodomew
**28.** kako~
**30.** elpi~

# Crossword Puzzle: Vocabulary Lists 22-24

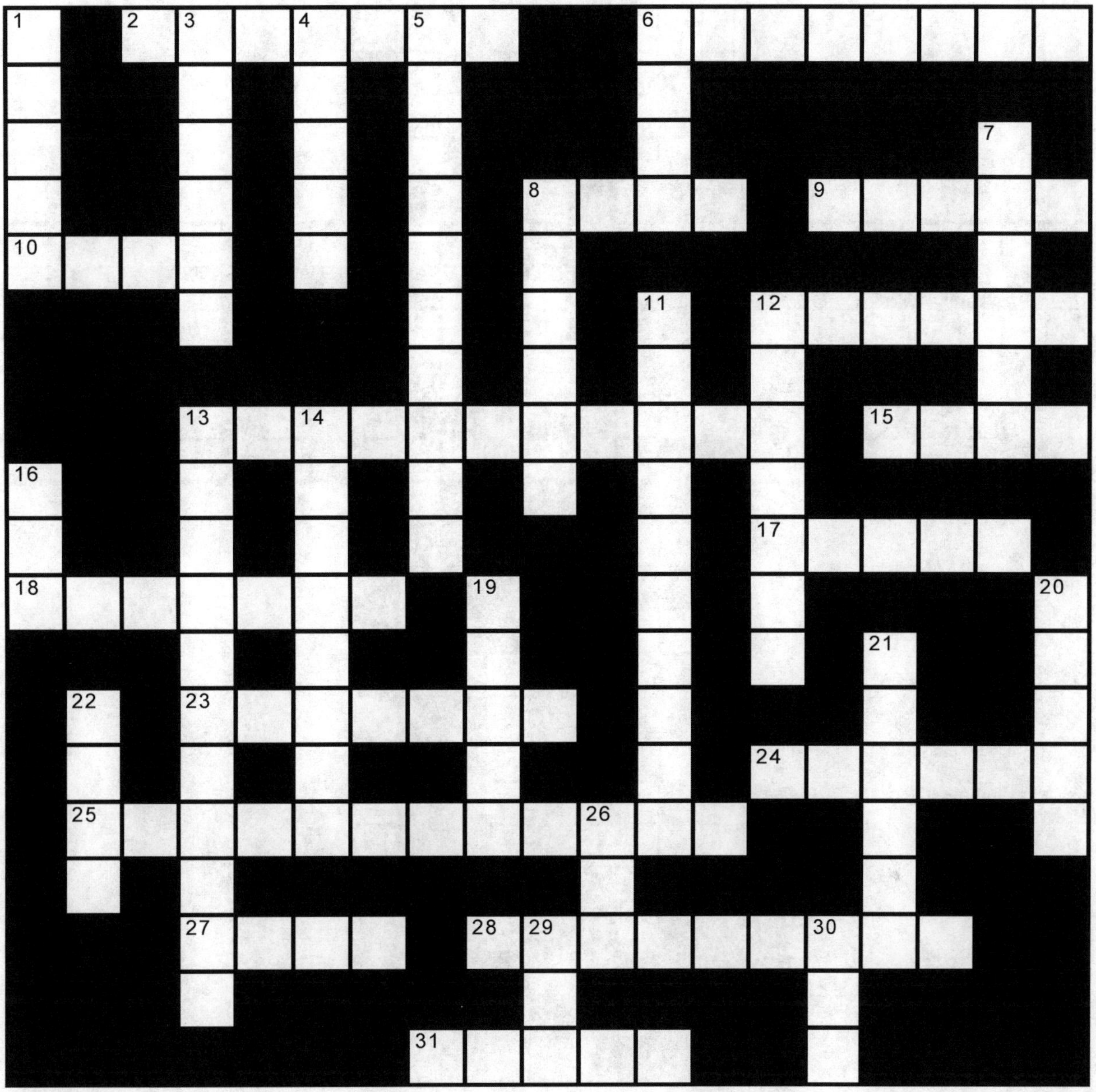

**Across**

**2.** epaggelia
**6.** opo~
**8.** w~
**9.** dunami~
**10.** wde
**12.** fulakh
**13.** eucaristew
**15.** sperma
**17.** dew
**18.** osti~
**23.** qaumazw
**24.** katoikew
**25.** men
**27.** omoio~
**28.** qhrion
**31.** ergazomai

**Down**

**1.** aptomai
**3.** mallon
**4.** stoma
**5.** ikano~
**6.** pleiwn
**7.** pro
**8.** axio~
**11.** genea
**12.** epiqumia
**13.** euqu~
**14.** etoimazw
**16.** op~
**19.** pou~
**20.** fwnew
**21.** pantote
**22.** qura
**26.** apa~
**29.** prassw
**30.** te

## Jumbo Crossword for Review: Vocabulary Lists 1-25

**Across**

**1.** deutero~
**4.** ei
**5.** allo~
**6.** daimonion
**7.** telo~
**9.** mero~
**10.** anhr
**12.** ekasto~
**14.** kako~
**18.** logizomai
**20.** aptomai
**22.** su
**23.** gh
**25.** ponhro~
**26.** amartia
**27.** umei~
**28.** dia
**31.** nekro~
**32.** oso~
**33.** trei~
**34.** apa~
**36.** mallon
**38.** outo~
**39.** qura
**41.** en
**42.** ceir
**43.** o~
**44.** ei~

**Down**

**1.** sperma
**2.** entolh
**3.** oudei~
**4.** blepw
**8.** qanato~
**9.** iereu~
**10.** wra
**11.** upo
**13.** ekklhsia
**14.** opisw
**15.** hmera
**16.** tiqhmi
**17.** oun
**19.** poli~
**21.** kefalh
**24.** duo
**29.** ourano~
**30.** euaggelion
**32.** exousia
**34.** hdh
**35.** presbutero~
**37.** trito~
**40.** ek
**41.** prassw
**42.** auto~
**43.** hmei~

## Some Big Little "o" Words: ou & oti

You may remember that the letter omega (w) received its name by virtue of the fact that it is the longer, bigger "o" (o-mega), while the other "o" is small (Gk mikro~) and so it is called o-micron. Although it may be shorter in sound, the letter omicron begins two little words that have big implications in the Greek language.

### ou: The Sound of Negation

There are two primary ways to negate an assertion in Greek: use of the word ou, or use of the word mh. If someone *really* wanted to *emphatically* negate a statement, they might even use both! (cf. Mark 9:1, 41; 10:15; 13:2, 19; et al.)

Most of the time, readers of New Testament Greek will encounter the negation ou. It occurs about 1,619 times in the texts. However, the word ou poses problems for the ancient Greeks, who apparently did not like to pronounce two vowel sounds in succession (e.g. "ou akouete"). Wherever possible, they strove to eliminate this "awkwardness," which was even dubbed with it own Latin name: *hiatus*. So we have not one, but three forms of the word ou.

When the word following ou begins with a smooth, unaspirated vowel, ou takes the form **ouk**.

When the word following ou begins with an aspirated vowel (as though it started with the letter "h"), ou takes the form **ouc**. So:

οὐ νηστεύουσιν
They do not fast
οὐκ εἰμὶ ἱκανός
I am not worthy
**...**οὐχ ὁ ἄνθρωπος διὰ τὸ σάββατον·
...not humankind for the Sabbath.

The word mh is used when a verb is not in the indicative mood. It negates commands, infinitives, subjunctives, and the like. When you see the word mh (which occurs 1,055 times in the New Testament!), you know that the verb it negates is most likely NOT in the indicative mood (i.e. making a simple statement).

You might begin to ask: "What mood ***is*** this verb in?" We'll be exploring other moods later in the course.

Finally, note that the words ou and mh negate verbs. 1. Given this function, what part of speech are they? ___________

### oti: *because, that* or " "

When you come across the little word **oti** in the writings of the New Testament (in one of its approx. 1,280 manifestations), try three possible approaches: translate the word **because** or **that** or don't translate it at all, but simply introduce quotation marks into the sentence.

The word oti frequently has a causal meaning and can be translated **because**, as in the statement:

Λεγιὼν ὄνομά μοι, ὅτι πολλοί ἐσμεν.
My name is Legion, because we are many.

However, just as often oti is used to introduce *indirect discourse*. Indirect discourse is the embedding of a statement or a thought within another sentence. This statement has its own subject and verb within the confines of the sentence that contains the statement.

Some examples will help clarify. If we were to have the opportunity to learn directly from some ancient Jewish scribes, they might say "Elijah must come first." This would be a direct statement.

Later on, we discuss this teaching amongst ourselves, placing it into *indirect discourse*:

Dia ti λέγουσιν οἱ γραμματεῖς ὅτι Ἠλίαν δεῖ ἐλθεῖν πρῶτον;
Why do the scribes say **that** Elijah must come first?

Now the whole phrase "Elijah must come first" is functioning as a *noun clause*, performing the function of a noun in the main sentence "Why do the scribes say *x*?" It is when we find such a noun clause introduced by oti that we simply translate the word as "that."

Finally, we might not even translate the word oti at all! When this word is used to introduce direct discourse, the use of quotation marks is sufficient:

λέγουσιν αὐτῷ ὅτι Πάντες ζητοῦσίν σε.
They say to him, "Everyone is searching for you."

So mark this "dictionary entry" in your own personal vocabulary list: oti: because, that, "".

## The Big Little Words: ou and oti

Translate the following sentences as found in the Gospel of Mark. Helps are occasionally provided.

1. legei o anqrwpo~ τοῖς μαθηταῖς (of him) αὐτοῦ καὶ τῷ Πέτρῳ ὅτι o Ihsou~ προάξει (them) autou~ εἰς τὴν Γαλιλαίαν. ______________________________

______________________________

______________________________

2. khrussei ὅτι Ἐγὼ καταλύσω τὸν ναόν. ______________________________

______________________________

3. πάντοτε γὰρ τοὺς πτωχοὺς ἔχετε..., (me) ἐμὲ δὲ οὐ πάντοτε ἔχετε. ______________________________

______________________________

______________________________

4. οὐκ ἔστιν θεὸς νεκρῶν. ______________________________

5. ὁ υἱὸς τοῦ ἀνθρώπου ὑπάγει καθὼς grafousin (G: him) περὶ αὐτοῦ, οὐαὶ δὲ τῷ ἀνθρώπῳ (through whom) δι' ου ὁ υἱὸς τοῦ ἀνθρώπου ("is betrayed") παραδίδοται. ______________________________

______________________________

______________________________

6. ὁ Ἰησοῦς didaskei ἐν τῷ ἱερῷ, Πῶς λέγουσιν οἱ (scribes) γραμματεῖς ὅτι ὁ Χριστὸς υἱὸς Δαυίδ ἐστιν; ______________________________

______________________________

______________________________

# Correlative Bingo!

Certain Greek pronouns, adjectives and adverbs are *correlated* to one another both in form and meaning. Note some of the patterns below[1]:

| Interrogative<br>*p* | Indefinite<br>*enclitic* | Demonstrative<br>*t-* | Relative<br>*“h”* | Indefinite/<br>Indirect Interrogative<br>op- |
|---|---|---|---|---|
| **poio~**<br>what sort? | **poio~**<br>of some sort | **toiouto~**<br>such | **oio~**<br>such as | **opoio~**<br>of whatever sort |
| **poso~**<br>how many?<br>how much? | **poso~**<br>of some quantity | **tosouto~**<br>so many,<br>so much | **oso~**<br>as many as,<br>as much as | **oposo~**<br>however many,<br>however much |
| **potero~**<br>which of two? | **potero~**<br>any one of two | **etero~**<br>the other of two | --- | **opotero~**<br>whichever of two |
| **pou**<br>where? | **pou**<br>somewhere | **ekei**<br>there | **ou, enqa**<br>where | **opou**<br>wherever |
| **poqen**<br>from where? | **poqen**<br>from somewhere | **ekeiqen**<br>from there | **oqen**<br>from where | **opoqen**<br>from wherever |
| **poi**<br>to where? | **poi**<br>to somewhere | **ekeise**<br>to there | **oi**<br>to where | **opoi**<br>to wherever |
| **pw~**<br>how? | **pw~**<br>somehow | **outw~**<br>in this way | **w~**<br>as | **opw~**<br>however |
| **pote**<br>when? | **pote**<br>at some time | **tote**<br>then | **ote**<br>when | **opote**<br>whenever |
| **ph**<br>by which way? | **ph**<br>in some way | **tauth, thde**<br>in this way | **h**<br>in which way | **oph**<br>in whatever way |
| **ti~, ti**<br>who? | **ti~, ti**<br>anyone | **outo~, ekeino~**<br>this one, that one | **o~, h, o**<br>who, which | **osti~**<br>whoever |

**Why** not make up **some** cards, write on balls **of some sort**, and spin **something in some way** to see **who** might win your own version of *Correlative Bingo*? Be sure that **whenever anyone** wins, **whoever** that may be, there is **some sort of** prize to be had!

[1] The chart derives from the correlatives presented on page 276 of Donald Mastronarde, *Introduction to Attic Greek* (Berkeley: University of California Press, 1993).

# Help with Nouns

*Illustrating the Cases*
*Memorizing the Declensions*
*The Third Declension Song*

## Illustrating the Cases

Working with you learned about the different cases, fill in the blanks below. Above a given word write both (a) the case in which these nouns would appear in Greek and supply (b) a brief explanation for the choice of the case.

1 a. ______________________ 2 a. ______________________

b. ______________________ b. ______________________

**John** is a **student**.

3 a. ______________________ 4 a. ______________________

b. ______________________ b. ______________________

He sees three **friends**. He holds the **book**

5 a. ______________________ 6 a. ______________________

b. ______________________ b. ______________________

**of one friend**. **To that friend**

7 a. ______________________ 8 a. **Vocative**[1]

b. ______________________ b. ______________________

he gives that **book**. "Hey, **John**!" says

9 a. ______________________

b. ______________________

the **friend**, "Thanks!"

1. At times in ancient Greek texts a distinct case occurs for purposes of directly addressing a person, place, or thing. Grammarians have labeled this case, whose form is most often identical to the nominative, as the **vocative** case.



This exercise derives from material developed by Leslie Threatte, Professor Emeritus of the University of California at Berkeley. Used with his kind permission.

# Memorizing the Declensions

Here are some memory aids you might find helpful for learning the endings of each of the declensions.

## THE SECOND DECLENSION

| The Second Declension | | | |
|---|---|---|---|
| Singular | N | -o~ | Lost |
| | G | -ou | your |
| | D | -w | own |
| | A | -on | love? |
| Plural | N | -oi | Join |
| | G | -wn | a newvillage or |
| | D | -oi~ | a noisy |
| | A | -ou~ | house! |

And don't forget the *iota subscript* under the dative singular (-W)….

## THE FIRST DECLENSION

| The First Declension | | | |
|---|---|---|---|
| Singular | N | -a | Had |
| | G | -a~ | past |
| | D | -a | bad |
| | A | -an | savings? |
| Plural | N | -ai | Gain |
| | G | -wn | a newvision from |
| | D | -ai~ | a daisy |
| | A | -a~ | vase! |

Again, there is an *iota subscript* under the dative singular (-a)….

## THE THIRD DECLENSION

The basic paradigm is summarized in the column on the left. A memory device is on the right:

| The Third Declension | | | |
|---|---|---|---|
| Singular | N | -~, # | The USA |
| | G | -o~ | costs a |
| | D | -i | big |
| | A | -a | tab. |
| Plural | N | -e~ | Test |
| | G | -wn | a newvirtue by |
| | D | -sin | u*sing* |
| | A | -a~ | cash! |

# The Third Declension Song

## Happy Birthday, πᾶσιν

*Paul Fullmer*

PARADIGM: THE THIRD DECLENSION

| | Masculine | Feminine | Neuter |
|---|---|---|---|
| **N**ominative | πᾶς | πᾶσα | πᾶν |
| **G**enitive | παντός | πάσης | παντός |
| **D**ative | παντί | πάσῃ | παντί |
| **A**ccusative | πάντα | πᾶσαν | πᾶν |
| **N**ominative | πάντες | πᾶσαι | πάντα |
| **G**enitive | πάντων | πασῶν | πάντων |
| **D**ative | πᾶσιν | πάσαις | πᾶσιν |
| **A**ccusative | πάντας | πάσας | πάντα |

# Help with Verbs

## Practice with Principal Parts: An Exercise

Complete the following chart by referring (1) to the section on "Principal Parts" in *Read Greek by Friday: A Beginning Grammar and Exercises* as well as (2) to pages 31-33, immediately following.

| # | a. Principal Part | b. Greek Verb Form | c. Tense | d. Voice | e. Translation |
|---|---|---|---|---|---|
| 1. | The sixth principal part of kaqarizw | | | | |
| 2. | | teqerapeumai | | | |
| 3. | | | | | "I will receive" |
| 4. | | gegrammai | | | |
| 5. | The fourth principal part of legw | | | | |
| 6. | | | | | "I was believed" |
| 7. | The second principal part of ferw | | | | |
| 8. | | | | | "I tempted" |
| 9. | | | | | "I have heard" |
| 10. | | | | | "I was preached" |
| 11. | | peponqa | | | |
| 12. | The fifth principal part of oraw | | | | |
| 13. | | hmarton | | | |
| 14. | | | | | "I will teach" |
| 15. | | eilhfa | | | |
| 16. | The first principal part of peirazw | | | | |
| 17. | | kekraga | | | |
| 18. | The third principal part of lambanw | | | | |
| 19. | | estrafhn | | | |
| 20. | | epoqhn | | | |

# The Principal Parts of 144 Verbs Frequently Found in the NT

The table that follows provides the basic principal parts for every verb in the New Testament that occurs more than fifty times in the New Testament. Also included on this list are certain verbs whose parts are particularly irregular. Principal parts that are unattested in ancient Greek are marked by three dashes.

| 1. Present Active | 2. Future Active | 3. Aorist Active | 4. Perfect Active | 5. Perfect M/P | 6. Aorist Passive |
|---|---|---|---|---|---|
| agapaw[2] | agaphsw | hgaphsa | hgaphka | hgaphmai | hgaphqhn |
| aggellw | aggelw | hggeila | hggelka | hggelmai | hggelqhn |
| agnoew | agnohsw | hgnohsa | hgnohka | hgnohmai | hgnohqhn |
| agw | axw | hgagon | hca | hgmai | hcqhn |
| airw | arw | hra | hrka | hrmai | hrqhn |
| aitew | aithsw | hthsa | hthka | hthmai | hthqhn |
| akolouqew | akolouqhsw | hkolouqhsa | hkolouqhka | --- | --- |
| akouw | akousw | hkousa | akhkoa | --- | hkousqhn |
| amartanw | amarthsw | hmarton | hmarthka | hmarthmai | hmarthqhn |
| anabainw | anabhsomai | anebhn | anabebhka | anabebamai | anebaqhn |
| anisthmi | anasthsw | anesthsa / anesthn | anesthka | anestamai | anestaqhn |
| anoigw | anoixw | anewxa | anewga | anewgmai | anewcqhn |
| apercomai | apeleusomai | aphlqon | apelhluqa | --- | --- |
| apoqnhskw | apoqanoumai | apeqanon | teqnhka | --- | --- |
| apokrinw | apokrinw | apekrinamhn | --- | apokekrimai | apekriqhn |
| apokteinw | apoktenw | apekteina | apektona | --- | --- |
| apollumi | apolw | apwlesa | apolwleka | --- | --- |
| apoluw | apolusw | apelusa | apoleluka | apolelumai | apeluqhn |
| apostellw | apostelw | apesteila | apestalka | apestalmai | apestalhn |
| aptw | ayw | hya | --- | hmmai | hfqhn |
| arneomai | arnhsomai | hrnhsamhn | --- | hrnhmai | --- |
| arcw | arxw | hrxa | hrca | hrgmai | hrcqhn |
| aspazomai | aspasomai | hspasamhn | --- | --- | --- |
| afihmi | afhsw | afhka | afeika | afeimai | afeiqhn |
| bainw | bhsomai | ebhn | bebhka | bebamai | ebaqhn |
| ballw | balw | ebalon | beblhka | beblhmai | eblhqhn |
| baptizw | baptisw | ebaptisa | --- | bebaptismai | ebaptisqhn |
| blepw | bleyw | ebleya | --- | --- | --- |
| boaw | bohsw | ebohsa | --- | --- | --- |
| boskw | boskhsw | eboskhsa | --- | --- | boskhqhn |
| bouleuw | bouleusw | ebouleusa | bebouleuka | bebouleumai | ebouleuqhn |
| boulomai | boulhsomai | --- | --- | beboulhmai | eboulhqhn |
| gamew | gamw | eghma | gegameka | gegamhmai | --- |
| gennaw | gennhsw | egennhsa | gegennhka | gegennhmai | egennhqhn |
| ginomai | genhsomai | egenomhn | gegona | gegenhmai | egenhqhn |
| ginwskw | gnwsomai | egnwn | egnwka | egnwsmai | egnwsqhn |
| grafw | grayw | egraya | gegrafa | gegrammai | egrafhn |
| deiknumi | deixw | edeixa | dedeica | dedeigmai | edeicqhn |
| decomai | dexomai | edexamhn | --- | dedegmai | edecqhn |
| diakrinw | diakrinw | diekrina | diakekrina | diakekrimai | diekriqhn |
| diastellw | diastelw | diesteila | diestalka | diestalmai | diestalhn |
| didaskw | didaxw | edidaxa | dedidaca | dedidagmai | edidacqhn |
| didwmi | dwsw | edwka | dedwka | dedomai | edoqhn |

[2] In Greek texts, this verb form occurs as agapw. First person singular forms of contract verbs are regularly shown uncontracted in dictionaries and paradigms.

## The Principal Parts of 144 Verbs Frequently Found in the NT

| 1. Present Active | 2. Future Active | 3. Aorist Active | 4. Perfect Active | 5. Perfect M/P | 6. Aorist Passive |
|---|---|---|---|---|---|
| dihgeomai | dihghsomai | dihghsamhn | --- | dihghmai | dihghqhn |
| diwkw | diwzomai | ediwxa | dediwca | --- | ediwcqhn |
| dokew | doxw | edoxa | --- | dedogmai | edocqhn |
| doxazw | doxasw | edoxasa | --- | dedoxasmai | edoxasqhn |
| dunamai | dunhsomai | --- | --- | dedunhmai | edunhqhn |
| eggizw | eggiw | hggisa | hggika | --- | --- |
| egeirw | egerw | hgeira | eghgerka | eghgermai | hgerqhn |
| eimi | esomai | --- | --- | --- | --- |
| eisercomai | eiseleusomai | eishlqon | eiselhluqa | --- | --- |
| ekballw | ekbalw | exebalon | ekbeblhka | ekbeblhmai | exeblhqhn |
| ekplhssomai | ekplhxomai | exeplhsamhn | --- | ekpeplhgmai | exeplaghn |
| elpizw | elpiw | hlpisa | --- | --- | hlpisqhn |
| exercomai | exeleusomai | exhlqon | exelhluqa | --- | --- |
| exestin | exestai | --- | --- | --- | --- |
| epitimaw | epitimhsw | epetimhsa | epitetimhka | epitetimhmai | epetimhqhn |
| ercomai | eleusomai | hlqon | elhluqa | --- | --- |
| erwtaw | erwthsw | hrwthsa | hrwthka | hrwthmai | hrwthqhn |
| esqiw | fagomai/edomai | efagon | edhdoka | edhdesmai | hdesqhn |
| etoimazw | etoimasw | htoimasa | htoimaka | htoimasmai | htoimasqhn |
| euaggelizw | euaggelisw | euhggelisa | euhggelika | euhggelismai | euhggelisqhn |
| euriskw | eurhsw | euron | hurhka | hurhmai | hureqhn |
| ecw | exw / schsw | escon | eschka | eschmai | --- |
| zaw | zhsw | ezhsa | ezhka | --- | --- |
| zeugnumi | zeuxw | ezeuxa | --- | ezeugmai | ezeucqhn |
| zhtew | zhthsw | ezhthsa | ezhthka | --- | ezhthqhn |
| hgeomai | hghsomai | hghsamhn | --- | hghmai | hghqhn |
| qaumazw | qaumasomai | eqaumasa | teqaumaka | teqaumasmai | eqaumasqhn |
| qelw | qelhsw | hqelhsa | hqelhka | --- | --- |
| qerapeuw | qerapeusw | eqerapeusa | teqerapeuka | teqerapeumai | eqerateuqhn |
| qewrew | qewrhsw | eqewrhsa | --- | --- | eqewrhqhn |
| qorubew | qorubhsw | eqorubhsa | teqorubhka | teqorubhmai | eqorubhqhn |
| ihmi | hsw | hka | eika | eimai | eiqhn |
| isthmi | sthsw | esthsa / esthn | esthka | estamai | estaqhn |
| kaqarizw | kaqariw | ekaqarisa | --- | kekaqarismai | ekaqarisqhn |
| kaqeudw | kateudhsw | --- | --- | --- | --- |
| kaqhmai | --- | --- | --- | kaqhmai | --- |
| kaqizw | kaqiw/kaqisw | ekaqisa | kekaqika | --- | --- |
| kalew | kalw | ekalesa | keklhka | keklhmai | eklhqhn |
| katabainw | katabhsomai | katebhn | katabebhka | katabebamai | katebaqhn |
| katagelaw | katagelasomai | kategelasa | --- | --- | kategelasqhn |
| khrussw | khruxw | ekhruxa | kekhruca | kekhrugmai | ekhrucqhn |
| klaiw | klausw | eklausa | --- | --- | --- |
| krazw | kraxw | ekraxa | kekraga | --- | --- |
| kratew | krathsw | ekrathsa | kekrathka | kekrathmai | ekrathqhn |
| krinw | krinw | ekrina | kekrina | kekrimai | ekriqhn |
| kuliw | kulisw | ekulisa | kekulika | kekulismai | ekulisqhn |
| lalew | lalhsw | elalhsa | lelalhka | lelalhmai | elalhqhn |
| lambanw | lh[m]yomai | elabon | eilhfa | eilhmmai | elh[m]fqhn |
| legw | erw | eipon | eirhka | eirhmai | erreqhn |
| leipw | leiyw | elipon | leloipa | leleimmai | eleifqhn |

# The Principal Parts of 144 Verbs Frequently Found in the NT

| 1. Present Active | 2. Future Active | 3. Aorist Active | 4. Perfect Active | 5. Perfect M/P | 6. Aorist Passive |
|---|---|---|---|---|---|
| luw | lusw | elusa | leluka | lelumai | eluqhn |
| marturew | marturhsw | emarturhsa | memarturhka | memarturhmai | emarturhqhn |
| mellw | mellhsw | emellhsa | --- | --- | --- |
| menw | menw | emeina | memenhka | --- | --- |
| merizw | merisw | emerisa | memerika | memerismai | emerisqhn |
| metanoew | metanohsw | metenohsa | metanenohka | metanenohmai | metenohqhn |
| moicaomai | moichsomai | emoichsamhn | --- | --- | --- |
| xhrainw | xhranw | exhrana | --- | exhrasmai | exhranqhn |
| --- | eisomai | --- | oida | --- | --- |
| oraw | oyomai | eidon | eoraka / ewraka | ewramai | wfqhn |
| paradidwmi | paradwsw | paredwka | paradedwka | paradedomai | paredoqhn |
| parakalew | parakalw | parekalesa | parakeklhka | parakeklhmai | pareklhqhn |
| pascw | peisomai | epaqon | peponqa | --- | --- |
| peiqw | peisw | epeisa | pepeika/pepoiqa | pepeismai | epeisqhn |
| peirazw | peirasw | epeirasa | pepeiraka | pepeirasmai | epeirasqhn |
| pempw | pemyw | epemya | pepomfa | pepemmai | epemfqhn |
| peripatew | peripathsw | periepathsa | --- | --- | --- |
| perisseuw | perisseusw | eperisseusa | --- | --- | eperisseuqhn |
| pinw | piomai | epion | pepwka | pepomai | epoqhn |
| piptw | pesoumai | epeson | peptwka | --- | --- |
| pisteuw | pisteusw | episteusa | pepisteuka | pepisteumai | episteuqhn |
| plhrow | plhrwsw | eplhrwsa | peplhrwka | peplhrwmai | eplhrwqhn |
| poiew | poihsw | epoihsa | pepoihka | pepoihmai | epoihqhn |
| poreuomai | poreusomai | --- | --- | poporeumai | eporeuqhn |
| prassw | praxw | epraxa | pepraca | pepragmai | epracqhn |
| prosercomai | proseleusomai | proshlqon | proselhluqa | --- | --- |
| proseucomai | proseuxomai | proshuxamhn | --- | proshugmai | --- |
| proskunew | proskunhsw | prosekunhsa | proskekunhka | --- | --- |
| pwrow | pwrwsw | epwrwsa | pepwrwka | pepwrwmai | epwrwqhn |
| rhgnumi | rhxw | errhxa | errwga | --- | erraghn |
| riptw | riyw | erriya | errifa | errimmai | errifqhn |
| skandalizw | --- | eskandalisa | --- | eskandalismai | eskandalisqhn |
| speirw | sperw | espeira | --- | esparmai | esparhn |
| stenazw | stenasw | estenaxa | --- | --- | --- |
| strefw | streyw | estreya | --- | estrammai | estrafhn |
| sunagw | sunaxw | sunhgagon | sunhca | sunhgmai | sunhcqhn |
| swzw | swsw | eswsa | seswka | seswmai | eswqhn |
| threw | thrhsw | ethrhsa | tethrhka | tethrhmai | ethrhqhn |
| tiqhmi | qhsw | eqhka | teqhka | teqeimai | eteqhn |
| trecw | dramoumai | edramon | dedramhka | dedramhmai | --- |
| upagw | upaxw | uphgagon | uphca | uphgmai | uphcqhn |
| uparcw | uparxw | uphrxa | uphrca | uphrgmai | uphrcqhn |
| upotassw | upotaxw | upetaxa | upotetaca | upotetagmai | upetacqhn |
| ferw | oisw | hnegka | enhnoca | enhnegmai | hnecqhn |
| feugw | feuxomai | efugon | pefeuga | --- | --- |
| fhmi | fhsw | efhsa | --- | --- | --- |
| filew | filhsw | efilhsa | pefilhka | pefilhmai | efilhqhn |
| fobeomai | fobhsomai | efobhsamhn | --- | pefobhmai | efobhqhn |
| fulassw | fulaxw | efulaxa | pefulaca | pefulagmai | efulacqhn |
| cairw | carhsomai | ecarhsa | kecarhka | kecarhmai | ecarhn |

## "To Be" And Not "To Be"

The following selections from the Gospel of Mark illustrate a variety of uses of the verb eimi ("to be"). Increase your familiarity with this basic very by translating each. Helps are occasionally provided. Check your work against the solutions at the end of this volume.

(you will see)

1. ὁ δὲ Ἰησοῦς λέγει Ἐγώ εἰμι, καὶ ὄψεσθε τὸν υἱὸν τοῦ ἀνθρώπου. ____________

______________________________________________________________

(you) (speaking)

2. οὐ γάρ ἐστε ὑμεῖς οἱ λαλοῦντες ἀλλὰ τὸ πνεῦμα τὸ ἅγιον. ________________

______________________________________________________________

______________________________________________________________

3. ὧδε ἐν ἐρήμῳ τόπῳ ἐσμέν. ____________________________________

4. λέγουσιν ὅτι ἐν οἴκῳ ἐστίν. __________________________________

(of me)

5. Σὺ εἶ ὁ υἱός μου ὁ ἀγαπητός. _________________________________

6. ο κύριός ἐστιν ὁ υἱὸς τοῦ ἀνθρώπου καὶ τοῦ σαββάτου.

______________________________________________________________

7. οὐχ οὗτός ἐστιν ὁ τέκτων, ὁ υἱὸς τῆς Μαρίας καὶ ἀδελφὸς Ἰακώβου καὶ

(of him) (us)

Ἰωσῆτος καὶ Ἰούδα καὶ Σίμωνος; καὶ οὐκ εἰσὶν αἱ ἀδελφαὶ αὐτοῦ ὧδε πρὸς ἡμᾶς;

______________________________________________________________

______________________________________________________________

# Pick a Peck of Parsings

In each set below, match the correct verb from with the sentence to which it belongs. Then write out the translation on the line below. Use each word only once.

**1. speiretai speirei speiromen speirontai**

a. o speirwn ________________ tou~ logou~.

______________________________________________

b. kai to sperma ________________ upo tou speironto~.

______________________________________________

c. hmei~ ________________ sun tw speironti.

______________________________________________

d. oi logoi ________________ en toi~ ocloi~.

______________________________________________

**2. lousqhsontai louetai louontai louousin**

a. ta korasia ________________ ta imatia.

______________________________________________

b. ta korasia ________________ ta~ ceira~.

______________________________________________

c. ai skhnai ai uyhlai ________________ epaurion.

______________________________________________

d. h λευκὴ στολὴ ________________ en tw potamw.

______________________________________________

**3. akoush akousqhsetai akouete akousomeqa**

a. nun ________________ thn fwnhn;

______________________________________________

b. h fwnh sou ________________ en toi~ anqrwpoi~.

______________________________________________

c. th epaurion ________________ su thn fwnhn.

______________________________________________

d. eita ________________ kai hmei~.

______________________________________________

# Reproducible Parsing/Declension Form

| | VERB FORMS | | | | | | | | | | NOUN FORMS | | | | |
|---|---|---|---|---|---|---|---|---|---|---|---|---|---|---|---|
| | | | | | | | | For Participles | | | | | | | |
| Form in Text | 1st Principal Part | English Meaning | Pers | Num | Tense | Voice | Mood | Case | Num | Gen | Dictionary Entry Form | Case | Num | Gen | Decl |

# Parsing Flow Chart

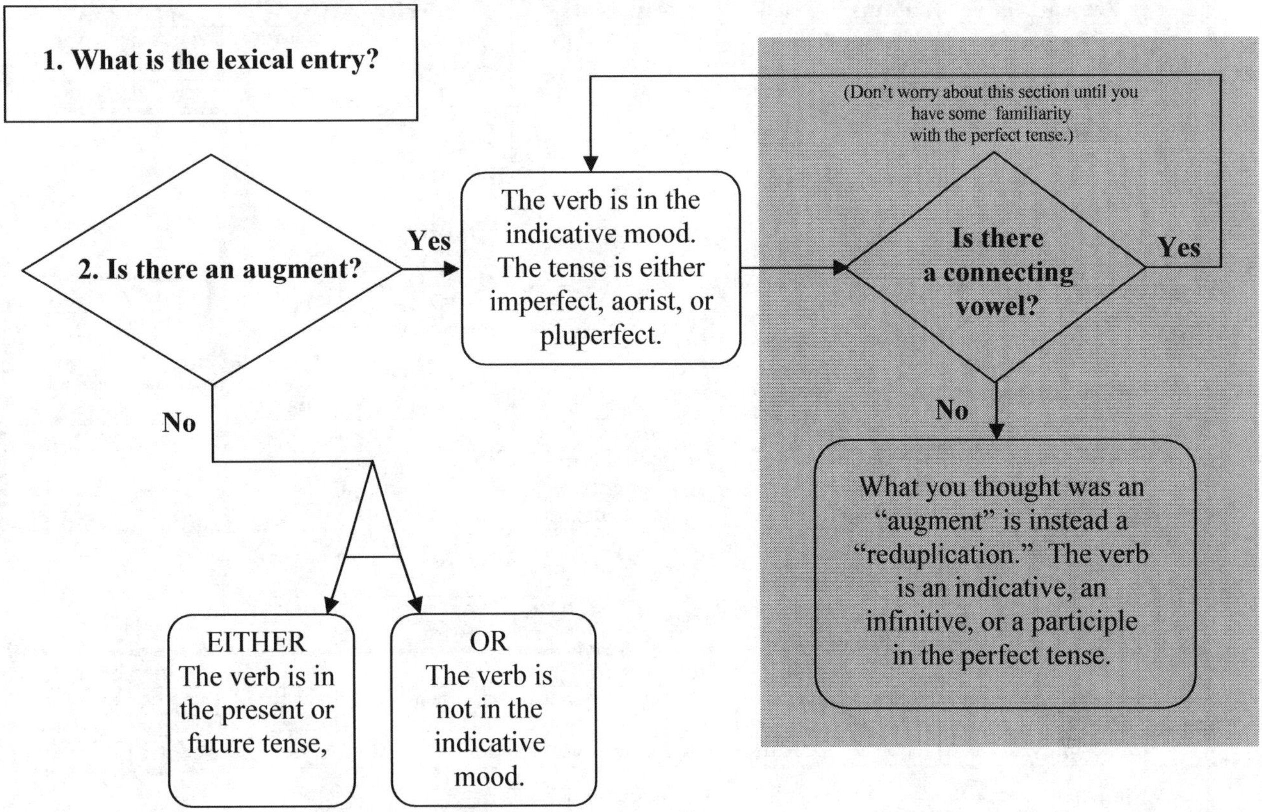


**3. What is the connecting vowel?**

| Connecting vowel | Tense | Voice |
|---|---|---|
| -ο/ε- | Pres/Fut | Act/ Mid/ Passive |
| | Impf | Act/Mid/ Passive |
| | 2 Aor | Act/ Mid |
| -α- | 1 Aor | Act/ Mid |
| | Perf | Act |
| -ει → | Pluperfect | Act |
| **None** | 1 & 2 Aor | Pass |
| | Perf | Mid/ Passive |

**4. What is the infix?**

| Infix | |
|---|---|
| -σ- | Future Act/Mid OR 1 Aor Act/ Mid |
| -θη- | 1 Aor Passive |
| -θησ- | Future Passive |
| -η- | 2 Aorist Passive |
| -ησ- | 2 Future Passive |
| -κ- | 1 Perfect Active |
| -κει- | Pluperfect Active |

**5. What is the personal ending?**

shows → person and
shows → voice

# Synopsis of grafw: The Greek Verb at a Glance

| | Present Active | Future Active | Aorist Active | Perfect Active |
|---|---|---|---|---|
| **Indic** | γράφω γράφομεν<br>γράφεις γράφετε<br>γράφει γράφουσιν | γράψω γράψομεν<br>γράψεις γράψετε<br>γράψει γράψουσιν | ἔγραψα ἐγράψαμεν<br>ἔγραψας ἐγράψατε<br>ἔγραψεν ἔγραψαν | γέγραφα γεγράφαμεν<br>γέγραφας γεγράφατε<br>γέγραφεν γεγράφασιν |
| **Subj** | γράφω γράφωμεν<br>γράφῃς γράφητε<br>γράφῃ γράφωσιν | --- | γράψω γράψωμεν<br>γράψῃς γράψητε<br>γράψῃ γράψωσιν | γεγραφὼς ὦ γεγραφότες ὦμεν<br>γεγραφὼς ᾖς γεγραφότες ἦτε<br>γεγραφὼς ᾖ γεγραφότες ὦσιν |
| **Opt** | γράφοιμι γράφοιμεν<br>γράφοις γράφοιτε<br>γράφοι γράφοιεν | γράψοιμι γράψοιμεν<br>γράψοις γράψοιτε<br>γράψοι γράψοιεν | γράψαιμι γράψαιμεν<br>γράψαις γράψαιτε<br>γράψαι γράψαιεν | γεγραφὼς εἴην γεγραφότες εἶμεν<br>γεγραφὼς εἴης γεγραφότες εἶτε<br>γεγραφὼς εἴη γεγραφότες εἶεν |
| **Infin** | γράφειν | γράψειν | γράψαι | γεγραφέναι |
| **Ptcp** | γράφων, -οντος<br>γράφουσα, -ης<br>γράφον, -οντος | γράψων, -οντος<br>γράψουσα, -ης<br>γράψον, -οντος | γράψας, -αντος<br>γράψασα, -ης<br>γράψαν, -αντος | γεγραφώς, -ότος<br>γεγραφυῖα, -ας<br>γεγραφός, -ότος |
| **Impv** | γράφε γράφετε<br>γραφέτω γραφόντων | | γράψον γράψατε<br>γραψάτω γραψάντων | γεγραφὼς ἴσθι γεγραφότες ἔστε<br>γεγραφὼς ἔστω γεγραφότες ὄντων |

| Imperfect Active | |
|---|---|
| ἔγραφον | ἐγράφομεν |
| ἔγραφες | ἐγράφετε |
| ἔγραφεν | ἔγραφον |

| Plupf Active Ind | |
|---|---|
| ἐγεγράφη | ἐγεγράφεμεν |
| ἐγεγράφης | ἐγεγράφετε |
| ἐγεγράφειν | ἐγεγράφεσαν |

| Plupf M/P Ind | |
|---|---|
| ἐγεγράμμην | ἐγεγράμμεθα |
| ἐγεγράψο | ἐγεγράφθε |
| ἐγεγράπτο | ἐγεγράντο |

| | Present M/P | Future Middle | Aor M | Perfect M/P |
|---|---|---|---|---|
| **Indic** | γράφομαι γραφόμεθα<br>γράφῃ γράφεσθε<br>γράφεται γράφονται | γράψομαι γραψόμεθα<br>γράψῃ γράψεσθε<br>γράψεται γράψονται | ἐγραψάμην ἐγραψάμεθα<br>ἔγραψω ἐγράψασθε<br>ἐγραψάτο ἐγράψαντο | γέγραμμαι γεγράμμεθα<br>γέγραψαι γέγραφθε<br>γέγραπται γεγραμμένοι εἰσίν |
| **Subj** | γράφωμαι γραφώμεθα<br>γράφῃ γράφησθε<br>γράφηται γράφωνται | — | γράψωμαι γραψώμεθα<br>γράψῃ γράψησθε<br>γράψηται γράψωνται | γεγραμμένος, -η, -ον ὦ γεγραμμένοι -αι, -α ὦμεν<br>γεγραμμένος, -η, -ον ᾖς γεγραμμένοι -αι, -α ἦτε<br>γεγραμμένος, -η, -ον ᾖ γεγραμμένοι -αι, -α ὦσιν |
| **Opt** | γραφοίμην γραφοίμεθα<br>γράφοιο γράφοισθε<br>γράφοιτο γράφοιντο | γραψοίμην γραψοίμεθα<br>γράψοιο γράψοισθε<br>γράψοιτο γράψοιντο | γραψαίμην γραψαίμεθα<br>γράψαιο γράψαισθε<br>γράψαιτο γράψαιντο | γεγραμμένος, -η, -ον εἴην γεγραμμένοι -αι, -α εἶμεν<br>γεγραμμένος, -η, -ον εἴης γεγραμμένοι -αι, -α εἶτε<br>γεγραμμένος, -η, -ον εἴη γεγραμμένοι -αι, -α εἶεν |
| **Infin** | γράφεσθαι | γράψεσθαι | γράψασθαι | γεγράφθαι |
| **Ptcp** | γραφόμενος, -η, -ον | γραψόμενος, -η, -ον | γραψάμενος, -η, -ον | γεγραμμένος, -η, -ον |
| **Impv** | γράφου γράφεσθε<br>γραφέσθω γραφέσθων | | γράψαι γράψασθε<br>γραψάσθω γραψάσθων | γέγραψο γέγραφθε<br>γεγράφθω γεγράφθων |

| Imperfect M/P | |
|---|---|
| ἐγραφόμην | ἐγραφόμεθα |
| ἐγράφου | ἐγράφεσθε |
| ἐγράφετο | ἐγράφοντο |

| | Future Passive | Future Perfect | Aorist Passive |
|---|---|---|---|
| **Indic** | γραφήσομαι γραφησόμεθα<br>γραφήσῃ γραφήσεσθε<br>γραφήσεται γραφήσονται | γεγράψομαι γεγραψόμεθα<br>γεγράψῃ γεγράψεσθε<br>γεγράψεται γεγράψονται | ἐγράφην ἐγράφημεν<br>ἐγράφης ἐγράφητε<br>ἐγράφη ἐγράφησαν |
| **Subj** | --- | --- | γραφῶ γραφῶμεν<br>γραφῇς γραφῆτε<br>γραφῇ γραφῶσιν |
| **Opt** | γραφησοίμην γραφησοίμεθα<br>γραφήσοιο γραφήσοισθε<br>γραφήσοιτο γραφήσοιντο | γεγραψοίμην γεγραψοίμεθα<br>γεγράψοιο γεγράψοισθε<br>γεγράψοιτο γεγράψοιντο | γραφείην γραφείημεν γραφεῖμεν<br>γραφείης γραφείητε γραφεῖτε<br>γραφείη γραφείησαν γραφεῖεν |
| **Infin** | γραφήσεσθαι | γεγράψεσθαι | γραφῆναι |
| **Impv** | --- | --- | γράφητι γράφητε<br>γραφήτω γραφέντων |
| **PTCP** | γραφησόμενος, -η, -ον | γεγραψόμενος, -η, -ον | γραφείς, -έντος<br>γραφεῖσα, -ης<br>γραφέν, -έντος |
| **Verbal Adj** | γραπτός, γραπτέος | | |

# Help with Accents

*Identifying Breathing Marks and Accents*
*Accenting Verbs*
*Accenting First and Second Declension Nouns*

Breathing marks can be hard to distinguish. Acute and grave accents as well! Here are some memory devices that may help….

## IDENTIFYING BREATHING MARKS

When a vowel or set of two vowels (a "diphthong") begins a word, it receives either a "smooth" breathing mark ( ) or a "rough" breathing mark ( ). A "rough" breathing mark ( ) has an *h* sound; a "smooth" breathing mark ( ) has none.

*Associating the marks with a stylized h may be helpful in learning this difference:*

☞ **tail points forward**

pronounce just like the letter "*h*"

which also has a tail that points forward

**ὁ = "hawe"**

☞ **tail points backward**

do *not* pronounce the letter "*h*",

just as the tail of the letter "*h*" does not usually point backward

**ὀ = "awe"**

## IDENTIFYING ACCENTS MARKS

There are three different accent marks in modern editions of Greek texts.

A *circumflex* accent is easy to identify because it has a *circular* shape:

῀

ᾶ ῆ ῶ οῦ

The second type of accent is called **the acute syllable** ( ´ ). This accent is only slightly different in form from the third type of accent, called **a grave accent** ( ` ). However, if you keep these images in mind, you might distinguish *a cute* accent from one that is very *grave*.

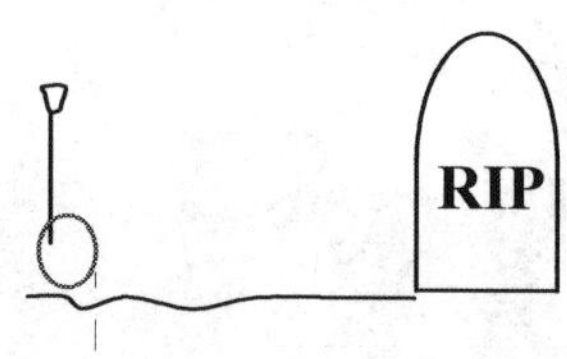

# Accenting Verbs: Recessive Accent Flow Chart

Basic familiarity with certain aspects of the accentuation system employed by most Greek texts will help you to identify contract verbs, verb forms, Greek composition and, in some cases, distinctly different verbs.

The standard system of accentuation printed in most modern, academic texts of the Greek New Testament[1] derives from the notation of scribes of the Byzantine Period.[2] In this system, vocal stress falls at the end of Greek words.

Most verb forms prefer a *recessive* accent: the accent moves back as far as possible: three "beats" from the end, where a short vowel typically receives one beat and a long vowel receives two.

Here is a flowchart you can use to determine the accentuation. Try is out on some of the verbs below. Then check your answers in the "Solutions" section at the back of the book.[3]

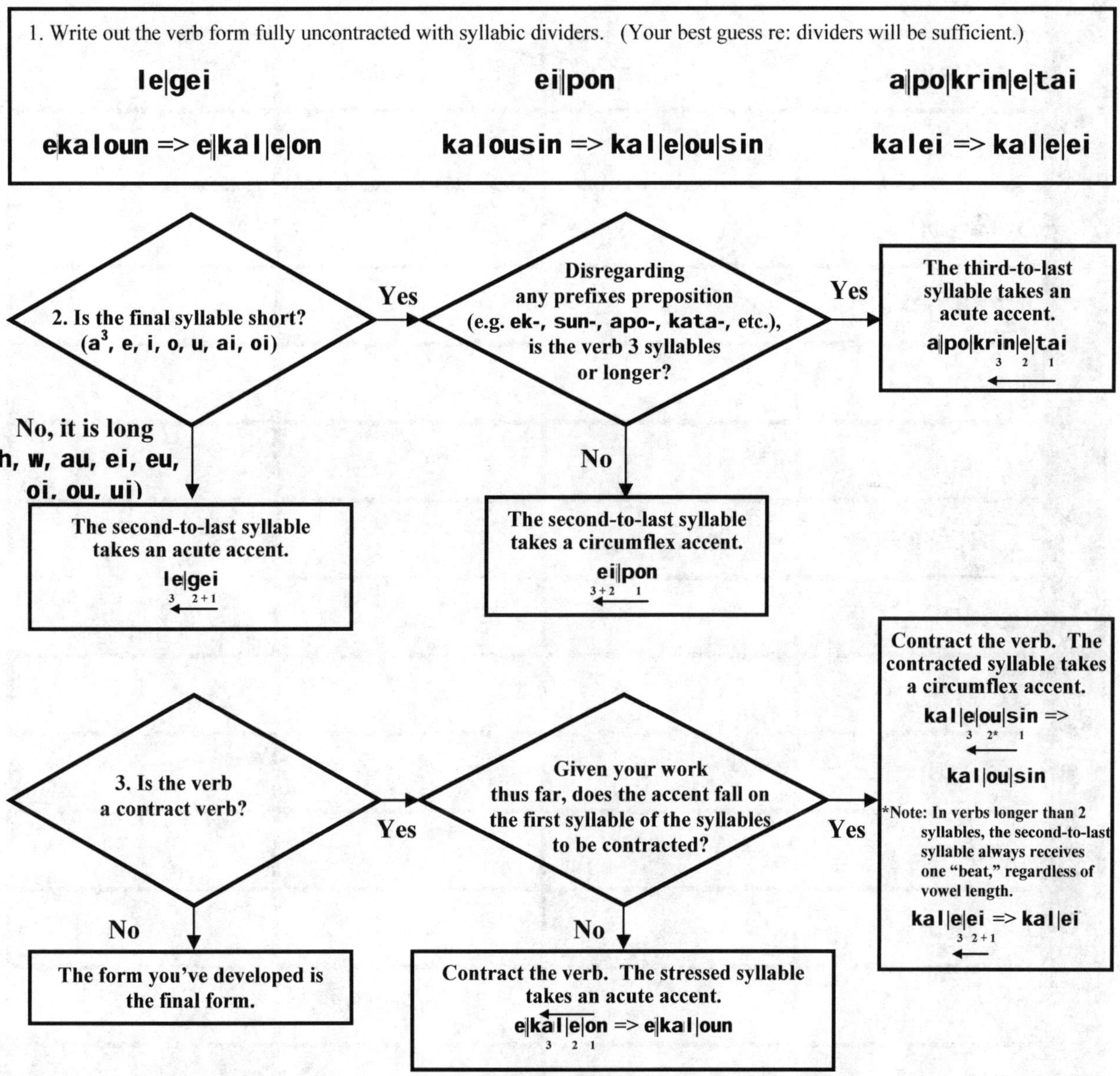


[1] See, for example, the two primary editions of the United Bible Societies (*The Greek New Testament* and *Novum Testamentum Graece*) as well as the Greek texts of the Loeb Classical Library and Oxford University Press.

[2] The earliest manuscripts to have any accent is the Cambridge manuscript (D), dated to the sixth century CE.

[3] The Greek vowel a is often long when following an i, r, or e. The vowels i and u can also, at times, be long.

## Accent on Verb Accents

Complete the following:

(1) If the verb in Column A is a contract verb, write out its uncontracted form in Column B
(2) Divide the verb form in Column A or B into syllables.
(3) Using the flowchart for accenting verbs, apply the appropriate accent to the word you have divided.
(4) If the word is a contract verb, write out its contracted form in Column C.
(5) Translate the verb into English in Column D

| | A | B | C | D |
|---|---|---|---|---|
| 1 | ποιειτε | | | |
| 2 | βαλητε | | | |
| 3 | κηρυσσω | | | |
| 4 | λεγεται | | | |
| 5 | συνηγον | | | |
| 6 | ἀποθνῃσκεις | | | |
| 7 | φαγωμεν | | | |
| 8 | ἐχεις | | | |
| 9 | agapwmen | | | |
| 10 | eidon | | | |
| 11 | apelusen | | | |
| 12 | σταυρουσιν | | | |
| 13 | ἠσαν | | | |
| 14 | ἐγραψα | | | |
| 15 | συναγω | | | |
| 16 | τιμωμεν | | | |
| 17 | λελοιπα | | | |

# Accenting First and Second Declension Nouns: A Flow Chart

Unlike most verbs, most nouns tend to have a stationary accent, placed within the last three "beats." In the majority of cases, the accent on a noun moves only when long endings are added to the end of noun, "pushing" the accent further back toward the end of a word:

nominative anqrwpo~ (3 2* 1 ←) => genitive anqrwpou (3 2+1 ←)

Experiment with the following flowchart and exercises to gain a sense for occasions when the accent of all noun shifts.

**1.** Write out (a) the form of the noun under consideration and (b) its dictionary form, both with their (likely) syllabic divisions:

______________________ ______________________

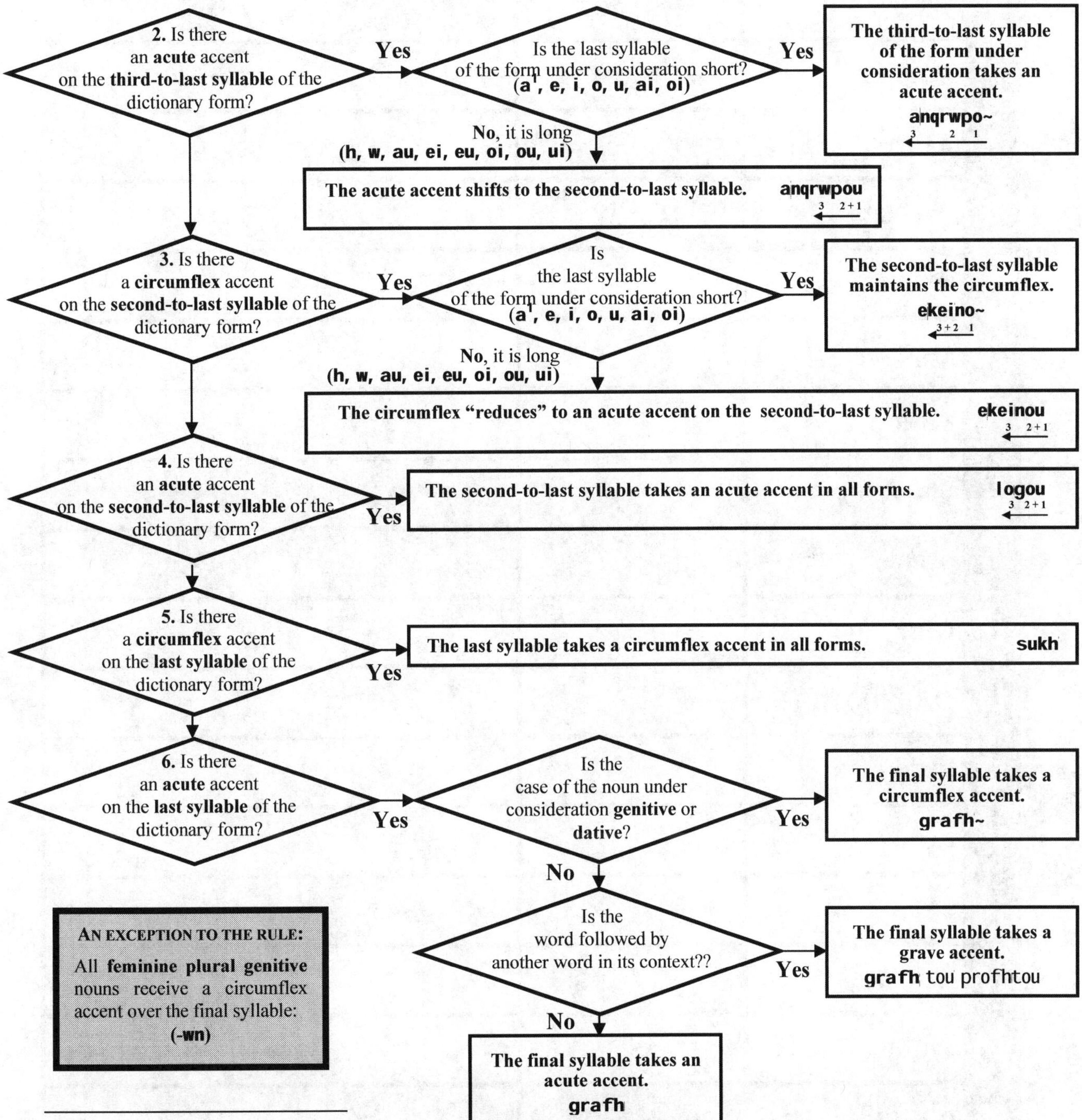


* As with verbs, so also in nouns longer than 2 syllables with accents in the dictionary form that recede to the third syllable, the second-to-last syllable receives one "beat," regardless of vowel length.

[1] The Greek vowel a is often long when following an i, r, or e. The vowels i and u can also, at times, be long.

## Accent on First and Second Declension Nouns

Complete the following exercise, progressing one number at a time:

(1) Begin in column A by dividing the noun form into syllables.
(2) In Column B, write the dictionary form and divide it into appropriate syllables.
(3) Using the flowchart for accenting nouns, apply the appropriate accent to the word in Column A.
(4) Translate the word form in Column A in Column C.

| | A | B | C |
|---|---|---|---|
| 1 | εὐαγγελιου | | |
| 2 | ποταμῳ | | |
| 3 | πλοιου | | |
| 4 | ἡμερων | | |
| 5 | θαλασσαν | | |
| 6 | κεφαλην αὐτοῦ | | |
| 7 | κεφαλην | | |
| 8 | ὑπηρεται | | |
| 9 | οἰνον | | |
| 10 | ghn | | |
| 11 | parabolhn | | |
| 12 | αὐτον καὶ | | |
| 13 | αὐτον | | |
| 14 | τελωνιων | | |
| 15 | ἁμαρτιων | | |
| 16 | αὐτῳ | | |
| 17 | οἰκιαν | | |

# A Memorization Project

*The Lord's Prayer*
*The Lord's Prayer Memorization Sheet*

# The Lord's Prayer from "Long, Long Ago"

One possible goal you might want to adopt for your work in New Testament Greek is to memorize some Greek... a song or poem you can take with you wherever you go once you have completed the course. Why not try to memorize the Lord's Prayer as it is written in the Gospel of Matthew (6:9-13)?

The following arrangement sets the Greek words of the prayer to the traditional song "Long, Long Ago." Sing the song through once before you begin each lesson, without worrying about declensions and conjugations. You'll be surprised how well you know it by the time the course is completed!

# The Lord's Prayer from "Long, Long Ago" (2)

## The Lord's Prayer from "Long, Long Ago": Memorization Sheet

Below is a copy of the text of "the Lord's Prayer" as it occurs in Matthew 6:9-13. The spacing and phrasing included are intended to help facilitate your memorization, in conjunction with the song.

Πάτερ ἡμῶν ὁ ἐν τοῖς οὐρανοῖς,
ἁγιασθήτω τὸ ὄνομά σου,
ἐλθέτω ἡ βασιλεία σου,
γενηθήτω τὸ θέλημά σου,
ὡς ἐν οὐρανῷ καὶ ἐπὶ γῆς.

Τὸν ἄρτον ἡμῶν τὸν ἐπιούσιον δὸς ἡμῖν
σήμερον·
καὶ ἄφες ἡμῖν τὰ ὀφειλήματα ἡμῶν,
ὡς καὶ ἡμεῖς ἀφίεμεν τοῖς
ὀφειλέταις ἡμῶν·
καὶ μὴ εἰσενέγκῃς ἡμᾶς εἰς πειρασμόν
ἀλλὰ ῥῦσαι ἡμᾶς ἀπὸ τοῦ
πονηροῦ.

# Class "Openers"

*The Doxology*
*"Let Us Worship"*
*Bless the Lord, O My Soul*
*Lord, Have Mercy*
*Shout with Joy to God*

## The Doxology

Class "openers" often ease the transition from extra-curricular life to an atmosphere of learning. This section introduces some sample prayers that may serve the purpose of an opening devotion while also providing further exposure to the Greek language.

α΄ Δόξα ἐν ὑψίστοις Θεῷ,
καὶ ἐπὶ γῆς εἰρήνη,
ἐν ἀνθρώποις
εὐδοκία

1) Glory to God in the highest,
and peace on earth,
goodwill between
people.

β΄ Δόξα ἐν ὑψίστοις Θεῷ,
καὶ ἐπὶ γῆς εἰρήνη,
ἐν ἀνθρώποις
εὐδοκία.

2) Glory to God in the highest,
and peace on earth,
goodwill between
people.

γ΄ Δόξα ἐν ὑψίστοις Θεῷ,
καὶ ἐπὶ γῆς εἰρήνη,
ἐν ἀνθρώποις
εὐδοκία.

3) Glory to God in the highest,
and peace on earth,
goodwill between
people.

δ΄ Κύριε, τὰ χείλη μου ἀνοίξεις
καὶ τὸ στόμα μου
ἀναγγελεῖ τὴν
αἴνεσίν σου.

4) Lord, open my lips
and my mouth
will proclaim
your praise.

ε΄ ᾿Αντιλαβοῦ, σῶσον,
ἐλέησον,
καὶ διαφύλαξον ἡμᾶς,
ὁ θεός, τῇ Σῇ χάριτι.

5) God, help us, save us,
have mercy on us,
and protect us
in Your grace.

## Let Us Worship

The Greek Orthodox Christian community uses a liturgical Greek in their worship that is very similar to New Testament Greek.[1] The subjunctive is the predominate mood in this prayer:

| | |
|---|---|
| Διδάσκαλος· | Teacher: |
| α′ Εὐλογητός ὁ Θεὸς ἡμῶν, | 1) Blessed is our God, |
| πάντοτε, | always, |
| νῦν, καὶ | now, and |
| εἰς τούς αἰῶνας τῶν αἰώνων. | forever and ever. |
| | |
| πάντες· | All: |
| β′ Δεῦτε, | 2) Come, |
| προσκυνήσωμεν καὶ | let us worship and |
| προσπέσωμεν τῷ | fall before the |
| βασιλεὶ ἡμῶν θεῷ. | King our God. |
| | |
| γ′ Δεῦτε, | 3) Come, |
| προσκυνήσωμεν καὶ | let us worship and |
| προσπέσωμεν | fall before |
| Χριστῷ, τῷ | Christ, the |
| βασιλεὶ, ἡμῶν θεῷ. | King, our God. |
| | |
| δ′ Δεῦτε, | 4) Come, |
| προσκυνήσωμεν καὶ | let us worship and |
| προσπέσωμεν | fall down before |
| αὐτῷ Χριστῷ, | Christ's very self, |
| τῷ θεῷ ἡμῶν. | our God. |

[1] I have adapted portions of the liturgy provided as "Weekly Bulletins for Worship in the Greek Orthodox Church" by the Greek Orthodox Church of the Assumption in Seattle, Washington. They are available on the Internet at http://students.cua.edu/16kalvesmaki/lit (June 1, 2004).

## Bless the Lord, O My Soul

a Eulogei h yuch mou ton Kurion,
kai panta ta ento" mou to
onoma to agion qeou.

1) Bless the Lord, O my soul,
and all that is within me,
bless God’s holy name.

b Eulogei h yuch mou ton Kurion,
kai mh epilanqanou
pasa" ta" antapodosei" qeou.

2) Bless the Lord, O my soul,
and do not forget
all of God’s benefits.

g Ainei h yuch mou ton Kurion:
ainesw Kurion
en th zwh mou:
yalw tw Qew mou,
ew" uparcw.

3) Praise the Lord, O my soul;
I will praise the Lord
while I live;
I will sing to my God
while I have my being.

d Makario", ou
o Qeo" Iakwb bohqo" autou,
h elpi" autou
epi Kurion ton Qeon.

4) Blessed is the one for whom
the God of Jacob is helper,
whose hope is
in the Lord God.

e Basileusei Kurio"
ei" ton aiwna,
o Qeo" sou, Siwn,
ei" genean kai genean.

5) The Lord will be king
forever;
your God, O Zion, will reign
throughout all generations.

z Eulogei h yuch mou ton Kurion,
kai panta ta ento" mou to
onoma to agion qeou.

6) Bless the Lord, O my soul,
and all that is within me,
bless God’s holy name.

# Lord, Have Mercy

| | |
|---|---|
| a O Qeo"<br>oiktirhsai hma"<br>kai eulogh sai hma" | 1) God,<br>be merciful to us<br>and bless us. |
| b Epifanai to proswpon sou<br>ef hma"<br>kai elehsai hma" | 2) Cause your face to shine<br>upon us<br>and be merciful to us. |
| g Tou en th gh<br>thn odon sou gnwnai<br>to swthrion sou<br>en pasin eqnesin | 3) That upon the earth<br>your way may be known,<br>your salvation<br>in all nations. |
| d Oi laoi, o qeo",<br>exomologhsasqwsan soi<br>laoi pante"<br>exomologhsasqwsan soi | 4) Let the nations, O God,<br>give thanks to you,<br>let all the nations<br>thank you. |

# Shout with Joy to God

a Allalaxate
tw Qew
pasa h gh.

b Yallomen dh
tw onomati sou
didomen doxan
ainesei sou.

g Legomen tw qew
w" fobera
ta erga sou.

d Pasa h gh
proskunhsatwsan soi
kai yalatwsan soi.

1) Shout with joy
to God,
all the earth.

2) We sing
to your name;
we give glory
for your praise.

3)We say to God:
'How awesome
are your works.'

4) Let all the earth
worship you,
and sing praises to you.

# Games

*Greek* BINGW
*Koine Combat*
*Closing Ceremonies*
*Creative Bibliography*

## Greek BINGW

Here's a fun way to celebrate the completion of this course, while continuing your Greek learning at the same time: play a few rounds of **BINGW**. To play, write out some New Testament verses (or as many words as you can), in Greek on a card such as this one:

# B I N G W

**VERSE:**

| | | | | | | |
|---|---|---|---|---|---|---|
| | | | | | | |
| | | | | | | |
| | | | | | | |
| | | | **topo~ eleuqero~** | | | |
| | | | | | | |
| | | | | | | |
| | | | | | | |

Then make a set of cards with categories such as:

> kai, *nominative* definite articles, adverbs, de, personal names, first or second person personal pronouns, numbers, plural definite articles, present active indicative verbs, aorist verbs, plural first declension nouns, plural second declension nouns, plural third declension nouns, singular first declension nouns, singular second declension nouns, singular third declension nouns, third declension adjectives, third person personal pronouns, prepositions, words of negations, subjunctive verbs, infinitives, imperatives, active participles, present or passive participles, middle or passive verbs, forms of eimi, -mi verbs, imperfect verbs, future verbs, verb forms in the perfect tense, any second singular verb, plural genitive nouns, neuter plural nouns, relative pronouns, words introducing a condition, aorist passive verbs, second aorist verbs, the word "God", middle/passive participles, aorist participles, gar, first declension adjectives, second declension adjectives, verbs with a prefix, verbs with an augment, nouns in the vocative case, interjections (e.g. "look!" "truly…"), demonstrative pronouns, singular dative nouns, words introducing a question, plural dative nouns, etc.

Call 'em out and see who is the first to get seven in a row diagonally, vertically, or on a diagonal. Keep track of what you call both on your card ("m&m's" work well!) and as a group (so you can verify that you have a winner). For the best participation, be sure the prizes are good!

## Koine Combat

Play "Koine Combat" if you are part of a learning group that is up for a little competition!

**Object**

The team with the highest points at the end of play wins.

**Preparing to Play**

(1) The instructor announces the domain of the upcoming game at the class session prior to play. The game might cover wide variety of domains, e. g. the aorist tense, forms of the verb didwmi and its compounds, second declension nouns, the definite article, etc.

(2) On the day of play, the instructor comes prepared with:
- A sheet outlining the paradigm to be tested,
- A pen,
- Several small slips of paper,
- A blank piece of paper for keeping score,
- A time piece that displays seconds, and
- A prize (optional; some suggestions: a box of cookies or candy for the team to share, pens, highlighters, etc.)

(3) The class is divided into equal teams of three to five students.

(4) Each team should have several small slips of paper and a writing implement.

**Round 1: Group Declension/Conjugation**

(1) Begin the first round by presenting (orally or in writing) the first group with a Greek word to be declined or conjugated (e.g. h|kousa).

(2) Working as a group, the team must produce all the proper declensional or conjugational components of the word within 10 seconds and submit it to the instructor (e.g. "first person aorist active indicative").
- If the team is correct, they receive one point. The instructor then presents the next word to this team.
- If the answer is not submitted on time or is wrong, no point is earned. Play transfers to the next group.

(3) Continue play in this manner until every team has had their turn as a group.

(4) At the end of Round 1, announce the current number of points held by each of the teams.

**Round 2: Individual Declension/ Conjugation**

(1) Beginning again with the first group, present (orally or in writing) one individual within that group a Greek word to be declined or conjugated.

(2) In a verbal response, the individual must produce all the proper declensional or conjugational components of the word within 10 seconds.
- If the individual is correct, record one point.
- If the individual is wrong, no point is earned. Play transfers to the next individual regardless.

(3) Continue play in this manner until every individual on every team has had their turn.

(4) At the end of Round 2, announce the current number of points held by each of the teams.

**Round 3: Group Form-Generation**

(1) Present (orally or in writing) the first group with a Greek declension or conjugation to be formed (e.g. "neuter plural dative of the definite article" or "third person singular aorist active indication of ercomai").

(2) Working as a group, the team must produce the proper form of the word within 10 seconds and submit it to the instructor (e.g. "toi~" or "hlqen"). Proper spelling counts; breath marks count; proper accentuation does not.

- ➢ If the team is correct, they receive one point. The instructor then presents the next word to this team.
- ➢ If the answer is not submitted on time or is wrong, no point is earned. Play transfers to the next group.

(3) Continue play in this manner until every team has had their turn as a group.

(4) At the end of Round 3, announce the current number of points held by each of the teams.

**Round 4: The Final Showdown!**

(1) Present (orally or in writing) the first group with a set of Greek declensions or conjugations to be formed (e.g. "the present active indicative forms of the verb eijmiv" or "all plural forms of the personal pronoun").

(2) Working as a group, the team must produce the proper forms of the word within 30 seconds and submit them to the instructor. Proper spelling counts; proper accentuation does not.

- ➢ In this round, the team receives two points for each correct answer. The instructor tallies and announces the points before proceeding to the next group.

(3) Continue play in this manner until every team has had their turn as a group.

(4) At the end of Round 4, announce the current number of points held by each of the teams beginning with the lowest score.

(5) The highest score is announced last, and takes the prize. Hopefully, however, they'll share any edible winnings with other class members as well!

# Ideas for a Greek Gala

*Some Creative Ways to Celebrate the Completion of this Coursework*

## Mediterranean Meal

Now that you've completed this stage in your process of learning Greek, why not end your class with a festive potluck? Many Mediterranean restaurants cater at a reasonable rate, offering Greek fare such as Souvlaki green salad, Orzo pasta salad, grape leaves and dolma, falafel, baba ghanoush with pita bread, hummus, feta cheese, assorted olives, and baklava for dessert. Perhaps you'd like to try to make some Greek dishes yourselves to share. A bottle of ouzo distributed in small cups will provide each student a celebratory "shot" in classic Greek style!

## Visit a Greek Orthodox Church or Retreat Center

Many Greek Orthodox Churches still consider the Greek language, both ancient and modern, as an integral part of their heritage and worship. Contact your local Greek Orthodox Church for information about your class attending a worship service as guests. Or, you might inquire about a tour of the facilities with an emphasis on the iconic and liturgical Greek displayed in the sanctuary and on the premises. A church representative may even be willing to share a brief lecture about the use of the Greek language within the Greek Orthodox Church. Such a shared experience has much to offer students interested in learning more about language, the church, and culture.

## Film Fest

Perhaps you'd like to with a movie as a group? Many enjoyable and educational films are available in video format through a local video rental store. On the lighter side, you might enjoy watching *Zorba the Greek* (1964), *The Greek Tycoon* (1978, also starring Anthony Quinn), *It's Not Easy Being Greek* (1998; comedy; a young man struggles with the tortures of love and cultural stereotypes while attempting to fulfill his family obligations during a three-night Greek festival) or *My Big, Fat, Greek Wedding* (2002; very funny; a young woman comes to appreciate the distinctiveness of her Greek culture). A classic documentary is Greek Testament (1942; directed by Alberto Cavalcanti).

## Some Greek Games

Greek "BINGO" and "Koine Combat" are described in Lesson 28. They are fun, interactive ways to incorporate more Greek learning in your celebration.

***Congratulations!***

# More Resources

***Other Creative Resources for New Testament Greek You Might Find Helpful***

Black, David A. *It's Still Greek to Me.* Grand Rapids, Michigan: Baker Book House, 1998.

Presents grammatical concepts (e.g. the semantics of Greek prepositions) in creative illustrations.

___________. *Using New Testament Greek in Ministry: A Practical Guide for Students and Pastors.* Grand Rapids, Michigan: Baker Book House, 1998.

Concrete recommendations for bridging the gap between exegesis and sermon.

Kubo, Sakae. *A Reader's Greek-English Lexicon of the New Testament.* Grand Rapids, Michigan: Zondervan Publishers, 1980.

Chapter-by-chapter vocabulary serves as a ready aid to the beginning reader.

Louw, J. P. and E. A. Nida. *Greek-English Lexicon of the New Testament: Based on Semantic Domains.* Minneapolis: Fortress Press, 1994.

Creative organization. Want to know all the Greek words in the New Testament that mean "righteousness"? Here's an easy way.

Metzger, Bruce M. *Lexical Aids for Students of New Testament Greek.* Third Edition. Grand Rapids, Michigan: Baker Book House, 1999.

Key vocabulary words are creatively sorted and indexed in several ways. A classic.

Robinson, Thomas A. *Mastering Greek Vocabulary.* Second Edition. Peabody, Massachusetts: Hendrickson Publishers, 1994.

Close attention to English cognates eases acquisition of vocabulary.

Scott, Bernard B., et al. *Reading New Testament Greek: Complete Word Lists and Reader's Guide.* Peabody, Massachusetts: Hendrickson Publishers, 1994.

Brief, simplified vocabulary paradigms for easy reference and review.

Wilson, Marvin R. and Chris A. Vlachos. *A Workbook for New Testament Greek: Grammar and Exegesis in 1 John.* Peabody, Massachusetts: Hendrickson Publishers, 1998.

Divides 1 John into twenty-five assignments averaging four verses.

# SOLUTIONS

# Solutions

**Page 3 Crossword: People and Places**

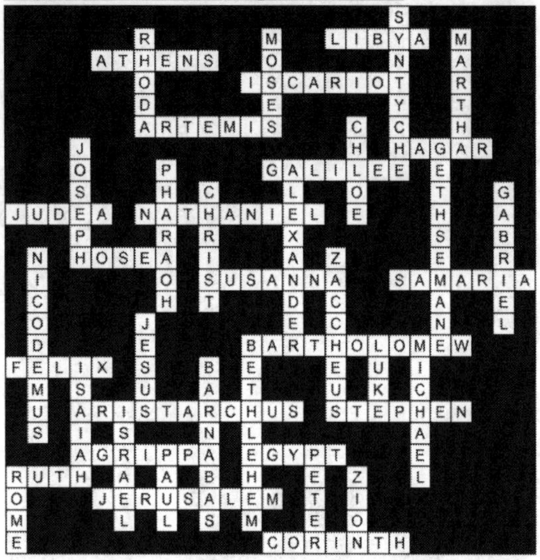

**Page 11 Crossword Puzzle: Vocab 1-3**

**Page 12 Crossword Puzzle: Vocab 4-6**

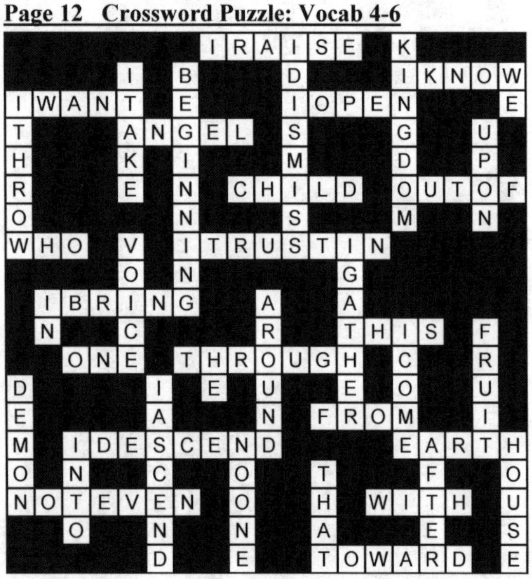

**Page 13 Crossword Puzzle: Vocab 7-9**

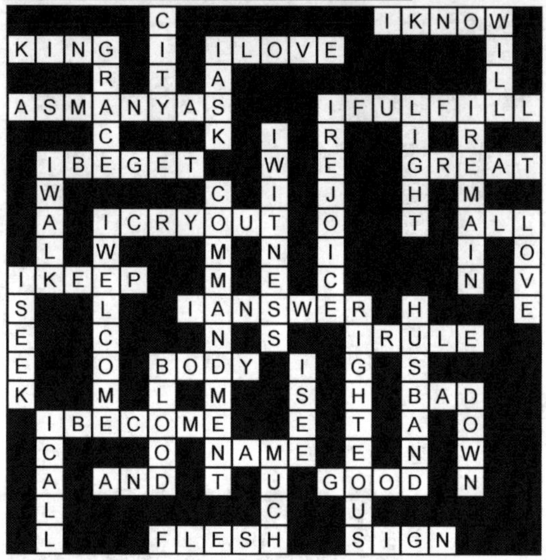

**Page 14 Crossword Puzzle: Vocab 10-12**

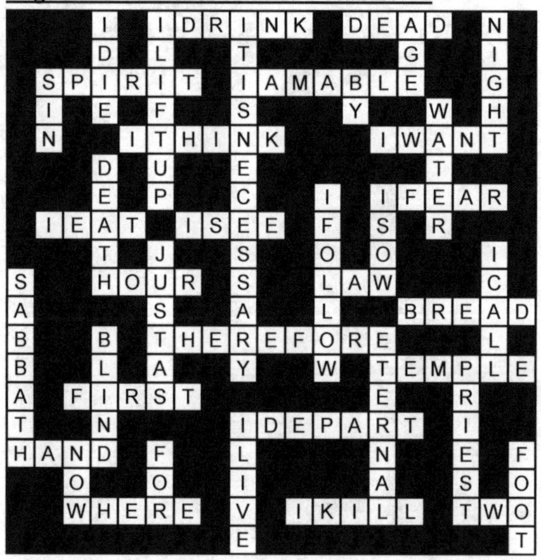

**Page 15 Crossword Puzzle: Vocab 13-15**

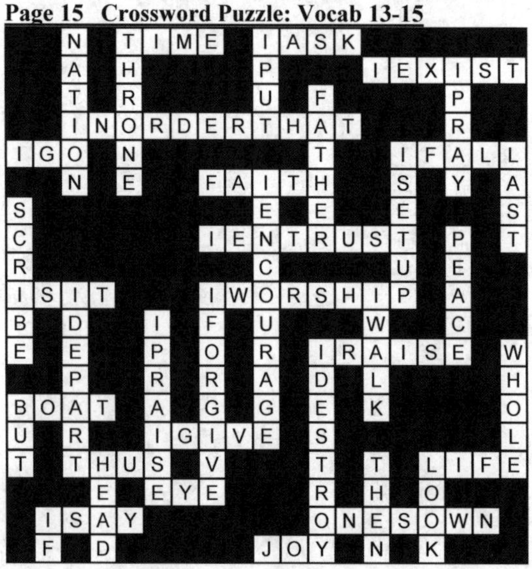

**Page 16 Crossword Puzzle: Vocab 1-15**

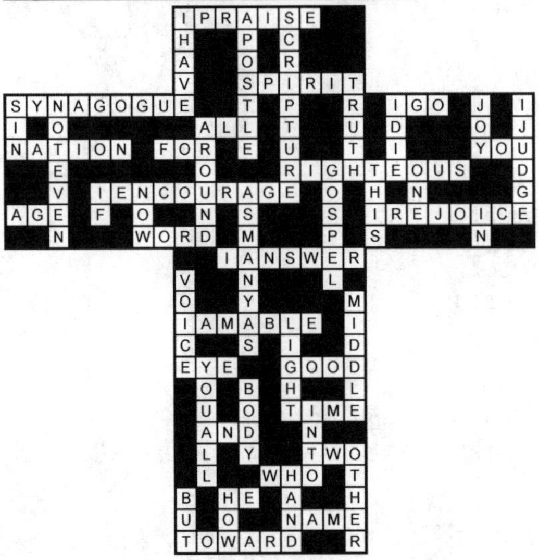

**Page 19 Crossword Puzzle: Vocab 22-24**

**Page 17 Crossword Puzzle: Vocab 16-18**

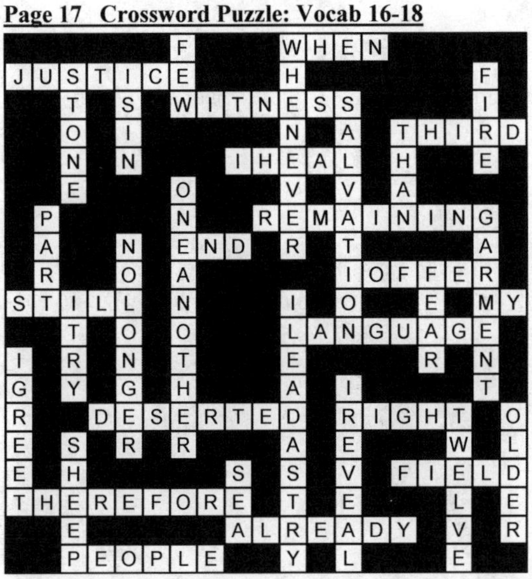

**Page 20 Crossword Puzzle: Vocab 1-25**

**Page 18 Crossword Puzzle: Vocab 19-21**

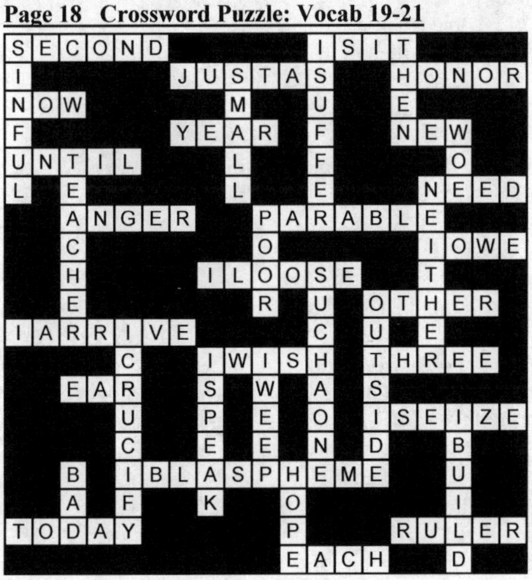

**Page 21 Some Big Little O-Words: ou & oti**

1. adverb

**Page 22 The Big Little Words: ou and oti**

1. The man tells his disciples and Peter that Jesus will go ahead of them to Galilee. (Mark 16:7)
2. He proclaims, "I will destroy the temple." (Mark 14:58)
3. "For you always have the poor, but you do not always have me." (Mark 14:7)
4. "He is not God of the dead."
5. "The Son of Man goes just as they write of him, but woe to the man through whom the Son of Man is betrayed."
6. Jesus teaches in the temple, "How do the scribes say that the Christ is a son of David?" (Mark 12:35)

# Solutions (3)

**Page 26 Illustrating the Cases**

1 a. nominative
b. subject of the sentence
2 a. predicate nominate
b. non-definitive equivalent of subject
3 a. accusative
b. object of verb "to see"
4 a. accusative
b. object of verb "to hold"
5 a. genitive
b. denotes possession
6 a. date
b. indirect object
7 a. accusative
b. object of verb "to give"
8 a. vocative
b. functions as address
9 a. nominative
b. subject of sentence

**Page 30 Practice with Principal Parts**

1 a. ---
b. ekaqarisqhn
c. Aorist
d. Passive
e. "I was cleansed"
2 a. The fifth principal part of qerapeuw
b. ---
c. Perfect
d. Middle/passive
e. "I have been healed"
3 a. The second principal part of lambanw
b. lhmyomai
c. Future
d. Middle (deponent)
e. ---
4 a. The fifth principal part of grafw
b. ---
c. Perfect
d. Middle/passive
e. "I have been written"
5 a. ---
b. eirhka
c. Perfect
d. Active
e. "I have said"
6 a. The sixth principal part of pisteuw
b. episteuqhn
c. Aorist
d. Passive
e. ---
7 a. ---
b. oisw
c. Future
d. Active
e. "I will bring"
8 a. The third principal part of peirazw
b. epeirasa
c. Aorist
d. Active
e. ---
9 a. The fourth principal part of akouw
b. akhkoa
c. Perfect
d. Active
e. ---
10 a. The sixth principal part of khrussw
b. ekhrucqhn
c. Aorist
d. Passive
e. ---
11 a. The fourth principal part of pascw
b. ---
c. Perfect
d. Active
e. "I have suffered/experienced"
12 a. ---
b. ewramai
c. Perfect
d. Middle/passive
e. "I have been seen" or "I have appeared"
13 a. The third principal part of amartanw
b. ---
c. Aorist
d. Active
e. "I sinned"
14 a. The second principal part of didaskw
b. didaxw
c. Future
d. Active
e. ---
15 a. The fourth principal part of lambanw
b. ---
c. Perfect
d. Active
e. "I have received"
16 a. ---
b. peirazw
c. Present
d. Active
e. "I tempt," "I test"
17 a. The fourth principal part of krazw
b. ---
c. Perfect
d. Active
e. "I have called out"
18 a. ---
b. elabon
c. Aorist
d. Active
e. "I received"
19 a. The sixth principal part of strefw
b. ---
c. Aorist
d. Passive
e. "I was turned," or simply "I turned"
20 a. The sixth principal part of pinw
b. ---
c. Aorist
d. Passive
e. "I was dranken"

**Page 34 "To Be" and Not "To Be"**

1. And Jesus says "I am, and you will see the Son of Man." (Mark 14:62)
2. "For you are not the ones speaking but the holy spirit [is the one]." (Mark 13:11)
3. "We are here in a deserted place." (Luke 9:12)
4. They report that he is at home. (Mark 2:1)
5. "You are my beloved son." (Mark 1:11)
6. "The son of man is lord even of the Sabbath." (Mark 2:28)

7. "Is this one not the carpenter, the son of Mary, and the brother of James, Joseph, Jude, and Simon? And are not his sisters here with us?"

**Page 35 Pick a Peck of Parsings**

1 a. speirei (PAI3S; The sower sows the words.)
b. speiretai (PPI3S; The seed is also sown by the sower.)
c. speiromen (PAI1P; We sow with the sower.)
d. speirontai (PPI3P; The words are sown among the crowds.)
2 a. louousin (PAI3P; The girls wash the clothes.)
b. louontai (PMI3P; The girls wash their hands.)
**NOTE: A middle sense is employed here because the girls are washing themselves. They are integrally involved in the process, washing "on their own behalf" as opposed to a direct object that is remove from themselves.**
c. lousqhsontai (FPI3P; The tall tents will be washed tomorrow.)
d. louetai (PPI3S; The white robe is washed in the river.)
3 a. akouete (PAI2P; Now do you hear the voice?)
b. akousqhsetai (FPI3S; Your voice will be heard among the peoples.)
c. akoush| (FMI2S; You will hear the voice on the next day.)
**NOTE: akouw is one of several verbs that have a deponent form in the future. See the chart of principal parts.**
d. akousomeqa (FMI1P; Then we also will hear.)

**Page 41 Accent on Verb Accents**

1 a. ποιειτε
b. ποι|έ|ετε
c. ποιεῖτε
d. "you do"
2 a. βάλ|η|τε
b. ---
c. ---
d. "you [should/might] throw"
3 a. κη|ρύσ|σω
b. ---
c. ---
d. "I preach"
4 a. λέ|γε|ται
b. ---
c. ---
d. "he/she/it is spoken"
5 a. συν|ῆ|γον
b. ---
c. ---
d. "I/they were gathering"
6 a. ἀ|πο|θνή|σκεις
b. ---
c. ---
d. "you kill"
7 a. φάγ|ω|μεν
b. ---
c. ---
d. "let us eat"
8 a. ἔχ|εις
b. ---
c. ---
d. "you have"
9 a. agapwmen
b. a|ga|pa|o|men [or a|ga|pa|w|men]
c. agapwmen
d. "we love" [or "let us love"]
10 a. eidon
b. ---
c. ---
d. "I/they saw"
11 a. a|pe|lu|sen
b. ---
c. ---
d. "he/she/it dismissed"
12 a. σταυρουσιν
b. σταυ|ρό|ου|σιν
c. σταυροῦσιν
d. "they crucify"
13 a. h|san
b. ---
c. ---
d. "they were"
14 a. ἔ|gra|ya or rewritten "ἔ|grap|sa "
b. ---
c. ---
d. "I wrote"
15 a. συ|νά|γω
b. ---
c. ---
d. "I gather"
16 a. τιμωμεν
b. τι|μά|ο|μεν or τι|μά|ω|μεν
c. τιμῶμεν
d. "we honor" or "let us honor"
17 a. λέ|λοι|πα
b. ---
c. ---
d. "I have left"

**Page 43 Accent on First and Second Declension Nouns**

1 a. εὐ|αγ|γελ|ί|ου
b. εὐ|αγ|γέλ|ι|ον
c. "of a gospel"
2 a. πο|τα|μῷ
b. πο|τα|μός
c. "to/for a river"
3 a. πλοί|ου
b. πλοῖ|ον
c. "of a boat"
4 a. ἡ|με|ρῶν **[NOTE the exception on page 42.]**
b. ἡ|μέ|ρα
c. "of days"
5 a. θά|λασ|σαν
b. θά|λασ|σα
c. "sea"
6 a. κε|φα|λὴν αὐτου
b. κε|φα|λή
c. "his head"
7 a. κε|φα|λήν
b. κε|φα|λή
c. "head"
8 a. ὑ|πη|ρέ|ται
b. ὑ|πη|ρέ|της
c. "servants"
9 a. οἶ|νον
b. οἶ|νος
c. "wine"
10 a. ghn
b. gh

c. “earth”

11 a. pa|ra|bo|l hn

b. pa|ra|bo|l h

c. “parable”

12 a. αὐ|τὸν καί

b. αὐ|τός

c. “him and”

13 a. αὐ|τόν

b. αὐ|τός

c. “him”

14 a. τε|λω|νί|ων

b. τε|λώ|νι|ον

c. “of tax-collectors”

15 a. ἁ|μαρ|τι|ῶν **[NOTE the exception on page 42.]**

b. ἁ|μαρ|τί|α

c. “of sins”

16 a. αὐ|τῷ

b. αὐ|τός

c. “to/for him”

17 a. οἰ|κί|αν

b. οἰ|κί|α

c. “household”